Revision Notes
for
Higher
Chemistry

D A Buchanan

(Faculty of Education,
University of Edinburgh)

J R Melrose

(Lenzie Academy,
Lenzie, Glasgow)

Published by
Chemcord
Inch Keith
East Kilbride
Glasgow

ISBN   1 870570 67 7

© Buchanan and Melrose, 1999
   First reprint 2002

Printed by Bell and Bain Ltd, Glasgow

Index

Note to students

The Course

- This book is designed to cover all of the content statements of the Higher Chemistry syllabus.

- Information relating to the Prescribed Practical Activities (PPAs) is included at the end of the book.

Your Revision

- Your revision is most likely to be effective if you stop at the end of each page and try to write out the main points.

- You can indicate your knowledge of each statement with a √ in the ❏ at the left hand side.

- Space has been left at the right hand side so that you can make additional notes.

- You can also mark statements with a highlighter pen.

- You are more likely to benefit from your revision if you work at a steady rate and follow a study plan.

- A time-table to help you plan your revision can be found on the next page.

- A lot of calculations in the Higher course involve simple proportion.
  There are a number of ways of laying out these calculations.
  Check with your mathematics teacher if you are unsure about the layout used in this book.

- A lot of the calculations in the revised Higher use numbers written as powers of ten,
  e.g. 9.65×10^4 which means 96 500.
  Again, check with your mathematics teacher if you are unsure about using your calculator for these calculations.

Study Planner

UNIT 1   Energy Matters

UNIT 2   The World of Carbon

UNIT 3   Chemical Reactions

PPAs

Unit 1   Energy Matters

1.   REACTION RATES

Rates of reaction

❏   the rate of reaction may be expressed in terms of the changes in concentration(s) of reactant(s) or product(s) in unit time

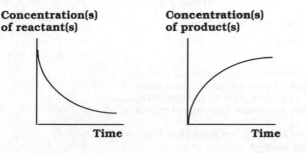

Concentration(s)
of reactant(s)

Time

Concentration(s)
of product(s)

Time

❏   the reaction rate is most rapid at the start of a reaction and decreases as the reaction proceeds

❏   when a change in concentration is measured in a given time expressed in seconds, the abbreviated unit of rate is mol l^{-1} s^{-1} (moles per litre per second)

❏   average rate of reaction = $\dfrac{\text{change in concentration(s) of reactant(s) or product(s)}}{\text{time taken for the change}}$

Example

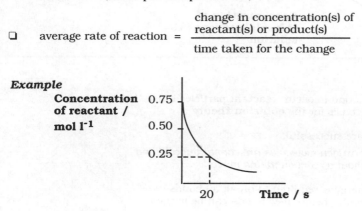

Concentration
of reactant /
mol l^{-1}

0.75

0.50

0.25

20   **Time / s**

The average rate of reaction over the first 20 s

is $\dfrac{0.75 - 0.25}{20}$ = $\dfrac{0.5}{20}$ =   **0.025 mol l^{-1} s^{-1}**

❏   since it is not always practicable to measure changes in concentration, changes in mass, in grams, and volume, in cubic centimetres, can also be used to measure rates of reactions; when changes are measured in a given time expressed in seconds, the abbreviated units are g s^{-1} and cm^3 s^{-1} respectively

Example

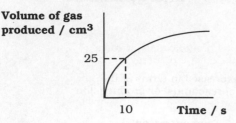

Volume of gas produced / cm³

25

10   **Time / s**

The average rate of reaction over the first 10 s

is $\dfrac{25 - 0}{10}$ = **2.5 cm³ s⁻¹**

❑   the rate of reaction is inversely proportional to time taken, i.e. the rate is proportional to "1/time taken"; this means that, for a fixed change in concentration, the shorter the time taken, the faster the rate of reaction

❑   for many reactions the rate is proportional to the concentration(s) of reactant(s),

> *e.g. the reaction between sodium thiosulphate solution and dilute hydrochoric acid to produce colloidal sulphur*

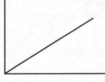

Rate

Concentration of thiosulphate ions in solution

Successful collisions

❑   for a chemical reaction to occur, reactant particles must collide; this is the basis for the **collision theory**

❑   not all collisions are successful,

> *e.g. nitrogen and oxygen molecules are constantly colliding in the air without a reaction taking place*

❑   this is because energy is required to break all bonds in the reactant molecules before new bonds can be formed,

> *e.g. the reaction of hydrogen with oxygen*

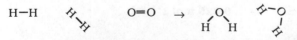

H—H   H—H   O=O   →   O / H H   H—O / H

energy needed to break bonds   **energy released in making new bonds**

- ❑ for a reaction to take place, reactant particles must collide with a certain minimum kinetic energy, known as the **activation energy**

- ❑ a fast reaction which occurs spontaneously at room temperature will have a low activation energy,

  e.g. $H^+(aq)$ + $OH^-(aq)$ → $H_2O(l)$

- ❑ the rate of a reaction which has a high activation energy can be increased if energy is supplied,

  e.g. *the reaction of nitrogen with oxygen in the air (from a spark), the reaction of hydrogen with oxygen (from a flame)*

- ❑ with some chemical reactions light can be used to increase the number of particles with energy greater than the activation energy,

  e.g. *an alkane reacts quicker with bromine in the presence of light*

Factors which affect reaction rate

(a) Concentration

See
UNIT 1 PPA 1

- ❑ as the concentration of a reactant increases the rate of collisions increases

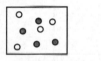 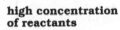

low concentration of reactants   **high concentration of reactants**

- ❑ this leads to an increase in the rate of successful collisions and hence reaction rate

(b) Particle size

- ❑ as the particle size decreases the surface area increases

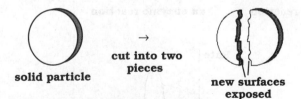

solid particle   **cut into two pieces**   **new surfaces exposed**

- ❑ collisions can occur on the new surfaces; this leads to an increase in the rate of successful collisions and hence reaction rate

(c) Temperature

See
UNIT 1 PPA 2

❏ the effect of temperature on reaction rate cannot just be explained on the basis of an increase in the rate of collisions with a rise in temperature

❏ temperature is a measure of the average kinetic energy of the particles in a substance

❏ if the temperature of a substance at T_1 is increased to T_2 then more particles will have energies which are equal to or higher than the activation energy, E_a

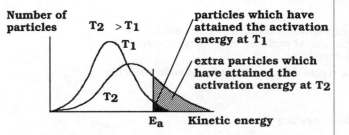

❏ this leads to an increase in the rate of successful collisions and hence reaction rate

❏ it is possible at low temperatures for no particles to have the activation energy and then no reaction occurs

❏ a small rise in temperature can cause a large increase in the number of particles having the activation energy and so can result in a large increase in reaction rate,

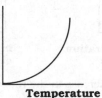

e.g. *for some reactions the reaction rate doubles for every temperature rise of 10 centigrade degrees*

❏ although most chemical reactions follow this pattern there are other possibilities,

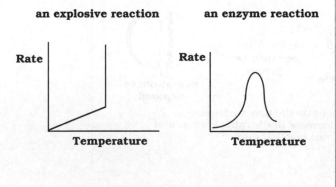

an explosive reaction   **an enzyme reaction**

Everyday examples

❑ there is a risk of explosions in flour mills and coal mines since the dust particles are very small (large surface area)

❑ bacterial action on food in a freezer is slower than in a fridge and hence it can be kept longer

❑ an oxyacetylene flame burns at a very high temperature due to the concentration of oxygen

Catalysts

❑ a catalyst speeds up a reaction by decreasing the activation energy

❑ more particles will have an energy equal to or in excess of the lower activation energy and hence be able to react

❑ this leads to an increase in the rate of successful collisions and hence reaction rate

❑ a catalyst takes part in the reaction but is **not** used up by the reaction

❑ a **heterogeneous catalyst** is one in which the reactants are in a different physical state from the catalyst

❑ reactions of gases often involve the use of a solid catalyst,

e.g. iron in the reaction of nitrogen with hydrogen, platinum in the reaction of ammonia with oxygen, vanadium pentoxide in the reaction of sulphur dioxide with oxygen

❑ reactant particles are **adsorbed** on to sites at the surface of the catalyst

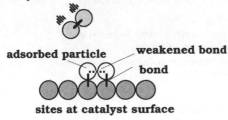

adsorbed particle — **weakened bond**

bond

sites at catalyst surface

❑ the bonds in the reactant particles are weakened and the particles are in favourable positions

❑ a collision is likely to be more successful than it would have been without a catalyst

- a reaction takes place and the product particles leave the catalyst surface

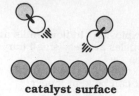

catalyst surface

- in many industrial processes catalysts are used to increase reaction rate,

    e.g. an iron catalyst is used in the Haber Process for the manufacture of ammonia

- **catalyst poisoning** can occur if impurities are adsorbed on to the surface of the catalyst taking up sites which could otherwise have been occupied by reactant particles

- industrial catalysts have to be **renewed** due to poisoning of the catalysts by impurities in the reactant; when the catalyst is renewed the 'spent' catalyst is removed and replaced by fresh catalyst

- some industrial catalysts which have been poisoned can be **regenerated**; this iinvolves 'cleaning' the catalyst by removing impurity from the active sites, usually by heating with a gas which reacts with the impurity,

    e.g. in catalytic cracking, air is used to burn off carbon from the catalyst

- catalytic converters are fitted to the exhaust systems of cars to catalyse the conversion of poisonous carbon monoxide and oxides of nitrogen in the exhaust gases to carbon dioxide and nitrogen; these gases are respectively produced by the incomplete combustion of the hydrocarbons in the petrol and the sparking of air

- cars with catalytic converters only use 'lead-free' petrol since lead poisons the platinum metal which is used as the catalyst

- a **homogeneous catalyst** is one in which the reactants are in the same physical state as the catalyst,

    e.g. cobalt ions in the reaction between potassium sodium tartrate and hydrogen peroxide

- a homogeneous catalyst takes part in the reaction and is then reformed at the end of the reaction

- **enzymes** catalyse the chemical reactions which take place in living cells of plants and animals,

    e.g. amylase in the breakdown of starch during digestion

- enzymes are highly specific in the reactions they catalyse, i.e. a particular enzyme will only catalyse a specific reaction or type of reaction

- enzymes are also important in industrial processes,

    e.g. zymase in yeast in the fermentation of sugars to alcohol

The mole - revision

❏ one **mole** (symbol mol) of any substance can be defined as the relative formula mass expressed in grams, i.e. the gram formula mass

❏ the **relative formula mass** of any substance is calculated from the formula using the relative atomic masses

❏ the relative formula mass has no unit, the relative atomic masses are measured relative to carbon-12

Example 1

Calculate the mass of 1 mol of sodium.

formula	Na
relative atomic mass	23
one mole	**23 g**

Example 2

Calculate the mass of 2 mol of hydrogen oxide.

formula	H_2O
relative atomic masses	(2 x 1) + 16
one mole	18 g
1 mol $\longleftrightarrow$	18 g
2 mol $\longleftrightarrow$	**36 g**

Example 3

How many moles in 10 g of calcium carbonate?

formula	$CaCO_3$
relative atomic masses	40 + 12 +(16 x 3)
one mole	100 g
100 g $\longleftrightarrow$	1 mol
10 g $\longleftrightarrow$	**0.1 mol**

❑ the concentration of an aqueous solution is the mass of solute dissolved in a certain volume of water

❑ concentration is usually expressed as grams per litre, symbol $g\ l^{-1}$, or moles per litre , symbol $mol\ l^{-1}$ ($mol\ dm^{-3}$)

Example 4

How many moles are there in 100 cm^3 of sodium hydroxide solution, concentration 0.4 $mol\ l^{-1}$?

$0.4\ mol\ l^{-1}$ is 0.4 mol in 1 litre

1000 cm^3 ⟷ 0.4 mol

100 cm^3 ⟷ **0.04 mol**

Example 5

What is the concentration of a solution of hydrochloric acid containing 0.1 mol in 50 cm^3?

50 cm^3 ⟷ 0.1 mol

1000 cm^3 ⟷ 2 mol

i.e. the concentration is **2 $mol\ l^{-1}$**.

Example 6

What volume of a sodium carbonate solution, concentration 2 $mol\ l^{-1}$, contains 0.5 mol?

2 $mol\ l^{-1}$ is 2 mol in 1 litre

2 mol ⟷ 1000 cm^3

0.5 mol ⟷ **250 cm^3**

Example 7

How many grams of hydrogen chloride are required to make 200 cm^3 of hydrochloric acid, concentration 2 $mol\ l^{-1}$?

Step A Calculate the number of moles required.

2 $mol\ l^{-1}$ is 2 mol in 1 litre

1000 cm^3 ⟷ 2 mol

200 cm^3 ⟷ <u>0.4 mol</u>

Step B Calculate the mass of one mole of hydrogen chloride.

> formula   HCl
>
> relative atomic masses   1 + 35.5
>
> one mole   <u>36.5 g</u>

Step C Calculate the mass of hydrogen chloride needed.

> 1 mol of hydrogen chloride has a mass of 36.5 g
>
> 1 mol   ⟷   36.5 g
>
> 0.4 mol   ⟷   **14.6 g**

i.e. **14.6 g** of hydrogen chloride are required to make 200 cm^3 of hydrochloric acid, concentration 2 mol l^{-1}.

Example 8

What is the concentration of a solution which contains 5.85 g of sodium chloride in 500 cm^3 of solution?

Step A Calculate the mass of one mole of sodium chloride.

> formula   NaCl
>
> relative atomic masses   23   +   35.5
>
> one mole   <u>58.5</u> g

Step B Calculate the number of moles of sodium chloride present in the solution.

> 58.5 g   ⟷   1 mol
>
> 5.85 g   ⟷   <u>0.1 mol</u>

Step C Calculate the concentration of the solution.

> 500 cm^3 ⟷   0.1 mol
>
> 1000 cm^3 ⟷   **0.2 mol**

i.e. the concentration of the sodium chloride solution is **0.2 mol l^{-1}**.

Calculations based on equations - revision

❏ a balanced equation can be taken to show the relative number of moles of each reactant and product

❏ since the mass of one mole of any substance is expressed in grams, the masses involved can then be calculated

Example 1

Calculate the mass of water produced on burning 1 g of methane.

balanced equation CH_4 + $2O_2$ → CO_2 + $2H_2O$

relative number   1 mol   2 mol
of moles

note: It is not necessary to calculate the masses of carbon dioxide and oxygen - these substances are not included in the question.

relative atomic masses CH_4 H_2O

                    12 + (4 x 1)   (2 x1) + 16

one mole   16 g   18 g

from equation   1 mol CH_4 ◄───► 2 mol H_2O

                        1 x 16g   ◄───► 2 x 18 g

                        1g   ◄───► 36 x $\dfrac{1}{16}$

                                =   **2.25 g**

Example 2

An industrial plant produces ammonia by the Haber Process. An output of 7.5×10^3 kg of ammonia is required each day.
Calculate the mass of nitrogen used each day assuming that the factory is working at 80% efficiency.

balanced equation N_2 + $3H_2$ → $2NH_3$

relative number of moles   1 mol   2 mol

relative atomic masses   (2 x14)   14 + (3 x 1)

one mole   28 g   17 g from equation 2 mol NH_3 $\longleftrightarrow$ 1 mol N_2

2 x 17 g $\longleftrightarrow$ 1 x 28 g

The plant is working at 80% efficiency,

hence 2 x 17 x $\dfrac{80}{100}$ g $\longleftrightarrow$ 1 x 28 g

7.5 x 10^3 kg $\longleftrightarrow$ $\dfrac{28 \times 7.5 \times 10^3 \times 100}{2 \times 17 \times 80}$

= **7.72 x 10^3 kg**

❏ when doing experiments with gases it is much more convenient to measure volumes than masses

Example 3

Calculate the volume of hydrogen produced when 0.2 g of zinc reacts with excess dilute sulphuric acid.
(Take the density of hydrogen to be 9 x 10^{-5} g cm^{-3}.)

volume of 1 mol of hydrogen

9 x 10^{-5} g $\longleftrightarrow$ 1 cm^3

1 mol (2 g) $\longleftrightarrow$ 1 x $\dfrac{2}{9 \times 10^{-5}}$

= $\underline{2.22 \times 10^4 \ cm^3}$

balanced equation

Zn + $H_2SO_{4(aq)}$ $\rightarrow$ $ZnSO_4$ + H_2

from equation 1 mol Zn $\longleftrightarrow$ 1 mol H_2

65.4 g $\longleftrightarrow$ 2.22 x 10^4 cm^3

0.2 g $\longleftrightarrow$ 2.22 x 10^4 x $\dfrac{0.2}{65.4}$

= **67.9 cm^3**

The idea of excess

❏ all reactants are needed for a chemical reaction to take place; when one of the reactants is used up the reaction will stop; any reactant which is left unreacted is said to be "in excess"

Example 1

8g of methane (CH_4) is mixed with 16 g of oxygen. A spark is applied to the mixture to start the reaction.

Calculate the mass of carbon dioxide produced.

balanced equation CH_4 + $2O_2$ → CO_2 + $2H_2O$

relative number
of moles   1 mol   2 mol   1 mol

methane   16 g ⟷ 1 mol

8 g ⟷ 0.5 mol

oxygen   32g ⟷ 1 mol

16g ⟷ 0.5 mol

Which reactant is in excess?

From the balanced equation,

1 mol of CH_4 reacts with 2 mol of O_2

0.25 mol of CH_4 reacts with 0.5 mol of O_2

Since there is 0.5 mol of CH_4, CH_4 is in excess.

Which reactant controls the mass of products?

Methane is in excess; the oxygen will all be used up; the mass of products will depend on the number of moles of oxygen.

Complete calculation

2 mol O_2 ⟷ 1 mol CO_2

64 g ⟷ 44 g

16 g ⟷ **11 g**

Example 2

What mass of hydrogen gas is produced when 2.43 g of magnesium is added to 100 cm^3 of dilute hydrochloric acid, concentration 1 mol l^{-1}?

balanced equation   Mg   +   2HCl(aq) $\rightarrow$ MgCl$_2$ +   H$_2$

realtive number   1 mol   2 mol   1 mol
of moles

     magnesium   24.3 g $\longleftrightarrow$ 1 mol

                        2.43 g $\longleftrightarrow$ 0.1 mol

     hydrochloric acid, concentration 1 mol l^{-1} has

                1000 cm^3 $\longleftrightarrow$ 1 mol

                100 cm^3 $\longleftrightarrow$ 0.1 mol

Which reactant is in excess?

From the balanced equation,

     1 mol of Mg reacts with 2 mol of HCl(aq)

     0.05 mol of Mg reacts with 0.1 mol of HCl(aq)

Since there is 0.1 mol of Mg, Mg is in excess.

Which reactant controls the mass of products?

Magnesium is in excess; the acid will all be used up; the mass of products will depend on the number of moles of acid.

Complete calculation

       2 mol HCl(aq) $\longleftrightarrow$ 1 mol H$_2$

          2 mol $\longleftrightarrow$ 2 g

         0.1 mol $\longleftrightarrow$ **0.1 g**

2. ENTHALPY

Exothermic and endothermic reactions

❑ an **exothermic** reaction releases energy, usually in the form of heat, to the surroundings

❑ the surroundings include the container in which the reaction takes place, the air round about and the reaction mixture itself

❑ if heat energy is released there will be a temperature rise in the surroundings since the latter absorbs the energy liberated by the reaction,

    e.g. the reaction between methane (CH_4) and oxygen (O_2)
          (burning of methane)

❑ a reaction in which energy is absorbed from the surroundings is called an **endothermic** reaction,

    e.g. the reaction between barium hydroxide pentahydrate
          ($Ba(OH)_2.5H_2O$) and ammonium thiocyanate (NH_4CNS)

❑ if heat energy is absorbed there will be a temperature fall in the surroundings

Enthalpy change

❑ every substance contains energy and its energy content is known as its **enthalpy** (H)

❑ enthalpy varies from substance to substance and so during a chemical reaction there is an enthalpy change (ΔH)

❑ the enthalpy change may be expressed as:

$$\Delta H \quad = \quad H_P \; - \; H_R$$

where H_P and H_R are the enthalpies of the products and of the reactants respectively

❑ while it is impossible to measure absolute enthalpies, it is possible to measure enthalpy changes, i.e. ΔH can be measured but not H_P or H_R

❑ enthalpy changes are usually quoted in kilojoules per mole of a reactant or per mole of a product, i.e. $kJ\ mol^{-1}$

❑ in an exothermic reaction the energy content of the product(s) is less than the energy content of the reactant(s)

❑ consequently the sign of ΔH is negative,

    e.g. $\Delta H = -50\ kJ\ mol^{-1}$

- in an endothermic reaction the energy content of the product(s) is greater than the energy content of the reactant(s)

- consequently the sign of ΔH is positive,
  e.g. ΔH = +25 kJ mol^{-1}

The path of a chemical reaction

- the bonds in the reactant molecules have to be broken; new bonds are then formed as atoms join up to form the product molecules

- a chemical reaction can be regarded as a series of bond breaking and bond making steps,
  e.g. burning of methane

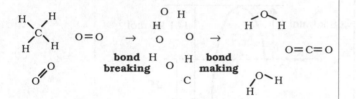

- energy is required to break the bonds in the reactant molecules but energy is released as new bonds in the product molecules are made

- the **activation energy (Ea)** for a reaction is related to the energy needed to break the bonds in the reactant particles

- if the total energy change for the bond beaking steps is less than that for the bond making steps, the overall reaction will be exothermic

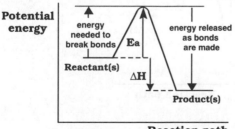

❏ if the reverse is true, then the reaction will be endothermic

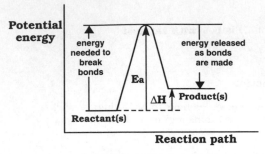

❏ an exothermic reaction can be illustrated

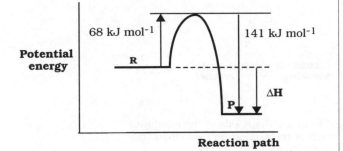

Ea = 68 kJ mol^{-1}
ΔH = -73 kJ mol^{-1}

❏ an endothermic reaction can be illustrated

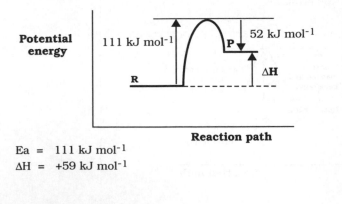

Ea = 111 kJ mol^{-1}
ΔH = +59 kJ mol^{-1}

❑ a catalyst speeds up a reaction by providing an
   alternative pathway with a lower activation energy

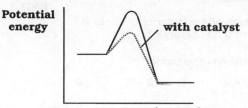

❑ because the activation energy is lower, more particles
   have the energy to react

❑ the enthalpy change for a reaction is **not** altered by the
   use of a catalyst

The activated complex

❑ the **activated complex** represents an intermediate stage
   between the reactants and the products,

   *e.g. the decomposition of a diatomic molecule XY into its
   elements*

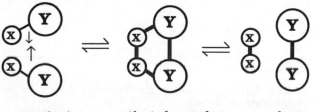

❑ the activated complex is formed at the top of the
   activation energy barrier and because of its high energy is
   very unstable

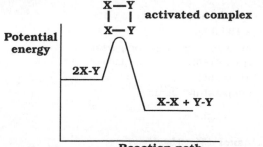

❑ the complex will lose energy and can fall back to the
   reactants side or fall forward to the products side

Enthalpy changes

(a) Enthalpy of combustion

See
UNIT 1 PPA 3

❏ the **enthalpy of combustion** of a substance is the heat given out when one mole of the substance burns completely in oxygen,

e.g. *the enthalpy of combustion of methanol*

$$CH_3OH_{(l)} + 1^1/_2O_{2(g)} \rightarrow 2H_2O_{(g)} + CO_{2(g)}$$

Example

Use the results below to calculate the enthalpy of combustion of ethanol.

Mass of burner at start	=	80.63 g
Mass of burner at end	=	80.48 g
Temperature of water at start	=	20.5 °C
Temperature of water at end	=	30.5 °C
Volume of water	=	100 cm³

Calculation

Mass of ethanol used	=	0.15 g
Rise in temperature	=	10 °C

It is assumed that the heat that is given out by the burning ethanol is taken in by the water in the can.

Heat released   =   c m ΔT

=   4.18 x 0.1 x 10

=   4.18 kJ

Note: c   =   specific heat capacity of water
=   4.18 kJ kg^{-1} °C^{-1}

m   =   mass of water absorbing heat
(1 cm³ of water has a mass of 0.001 kg)

ΔT   =   temperature change

Mass of one mole of ethanol (CH_3CH_2OH)
=   46 g

Heat released per mole of ethanol

0.15 g of ethanol $\longleftrightarrow$ 4.18 kJ

46 g (1 mol) $\longleftrightarrow$ 4.18 x $\dfrac{46}{0.15}$

= **1282 kJ**

Enthalpy of combustion of ethanol is **-1282 kJ mol^{-1}**.
(The sign is negative to indicate an exothermic reaction.)

❑ the enthalpies of combustion of some organic compounds are found on page 9 of the Data Booklet

Alcohol	Structural formula	Enthalpy of combustion/ kJ mol^{-1}
methanol	CH_3OH	-727
ethanol	CH_3CH_2OH	-1367
propan-1-ol	$CH_3CH_2CH_2OH$	-2020

❑ the experimental value is less than the value in the Data Booklet because it is assumed that all the heat energy from the burning is gained by the water; energy is however lost to the copper can and the surrounding air

❑ there is a fairly constant difference between the enthalpies of combustion for any two successive members of a homologous series; since each pair differ by a -CH_2- group the bond breaking energy and energy of bond making with oxygen is approximately constant for this group in different molecules

(b) Enthalpy of solution

❏ the **enthalpy of solution** is the enthalpy change which occurs when one mole of a substance is dissolved in water,

e.g. *the enthalpy of solution of sodium hydroxide*

$$NaOH_{(s)} \; + \; (aq) \; \rightarrow \; Na^+_{(aq)} \; + \; OH^-_{(aq)}$$

Example

When 2 g of sodium hydroxide is dissolved in 50 cm^3 of water at 20 °C the highest temperature recorded is 30 °C.

Calculate the enthalpy of solution of sodium hydroxide.

Heat released

$$\Delta H \quad = \quad c \; m \; \Delta T$$

$$= \quad 4.18 \times 0.05 \times 10$$

$$= \quad 2.09 \; kJ$$

Mass of one mole of sodium hydroxide (NaOH) = 40 g

Heat released per mole of sodium hydroxide

2g ⟷ 2.09 kJ

40 g (1 mol) ⟷ $\dfrac{40}{2}$ × 2.09

$$= \quad \textbf{-41.8 kJ}$$

i.e.

$NaOH_{(s)} \; + \; (aq) \; \rightarrow \; Na^+_{(aq)} \; + \; OH^-_{(aq)}$ **ΔH = -41.8 kJ mol^{-1}**

❏ in this calculation it is assumed that

(i) there is no heat loss to the surroundings,

(ii) the specific heat capacity of sodium hydroxide solution is the same as that of water

(c) Enthalpy of neutralisation

❏ when an alkali neutralises an acid, the hydrogen ions of the acid react with the hydroxide ions of the alkali

$$H^+(aq) + OH^-(aq) \rightarrow H_2O(l)$$

❏ the **enthalpy of neutralisation** is the energy released when one mole of water is formed in a neutralisation reaction,

e.g. the enthalpy of neutralisation of hydrochloric acid by sodium hydroxide solution

$$HCl(aq) + NaOH(aq) \rightarrow H_2O(l) + NaCl(aq)$$

Example

When 50 cm^3 of hydrochloric acid, concentration 1 mol l^{-1}, is neutralised by 50 cm^3 of sodium hydroxide solution, concentration 1 mol l^{-1}, at 20 °C the highest recorded temperature is 26 °C.

Calculate the enthalpy of neutralisation.

Heat released

$$\Delta H = c\ m\ \Delta T$$

$$= 4.18 \times 0.1 \times 6$$

$$= 2.52\ kJ$$

Number of moles of water formed

| 1000 cm^3 | ←——→ | 1 mol |

| 50 cm^3 | ←——→ | $\dfrac{50}{1000}$ x 0.1 |

$$= 0.05\ mol$$

Heat released per mole of water formed

| 0.05 mol | ←——→ | 2.52 kJ |

| 1 mol | ←——→ | $\dfrac{1}{0.05}$ x 2.52 |

$$= \mathbf{50.4\ kJ}$$

i.e. $HCl(aq) + NaOH(aq) \rightarrow H_2O(l) + NaCl(aq)$

$$\mathbf{\Delta H = -50.4\ kJ\ mol^{-1}}$$

❏ in this calculation it is assumed that
   (i)   there is no heat loss to the surroundings,
   (ii) the specific heat capacity of sodium chloride solution is the same as that of water,
   (iii) the density of sodium chloride solution is the same as that of water

❑ the enthalpies of neutralisation for all strong acids (nitric, hydrochloric and sulphuric) are very similar since the reaction is the same in each case

$$H^+(aq) \quad + \quad OH^-(aq) \quad \rightarrow \quad H_2O(l)$$

❑ the enthalpies of neutralisation for weak acids is less than for strong acids since energy is required to completely dissociate the weak acid molecules

3. PATTERNS IN THE PERIODIC TABLE

The modern Periodic Table

❑ the modern Periodic Table is based on the work of Mendeleev who arranged the known elements in order of increasing atomic weight but he also produced columns by placing elements with similar chemical properties the one below the other; in order not to destroy the pattern, gaps were left for elements yet to be discovered

❑ he made predictions about such elements,

   e.g. he correctly predicted the properties of the element germanium , an element he called eka-silicon

❑ in the modern Periodic Table each element in a period has an atomic number which is different by one from the preceding element; this reflects the difference in the number of protons in the nucleus of successive elements

❑ elements in the same group have the same number of electrons in the outer energy level (shell),

   e.g. the alkali metals have one electron in the outer energy level, the halogens have seven electrons in the outer energy level , the noble gases all have filled outer energy levels

❑ there are variations in the densities, melting points and boiling points of the elements across a period and down a group

Trends in the elements

(a) Atomic size

❑ **on crossing a period in the Periodic Table the atomic size decreases**

❑ on moving from one element to the next, electrons are being added to the same energy level and protons are being added to the nucleus; the electrons in the outer energy level are therefore attracted more strongly and pulled closer to the nucleus because of its increasing positive charge

❑ **on descending a group in the Periodic Table the atomic size increases**

❑ on moving from one element to the next, the number of occupied energy levels is increasing

❑ the atomic size is an example of a periodic property, i.e. with increasing atomic number there is a definite pattern which is repeated across a number of elements (a period), with elements in the same groups occurring at the same positions on the "waves"

(b) Ionisation energy

❑ the **first ionisation energy** of an element is the energy required to remove one electron from each atom in one mole of gaseous atoms of the element,

e.g. the first ionisation energy of potassium

$$K_{(g)} \rightarrow K^+_{(g)} + e^- \quad \Delta H = +425 \text{ kJ mol}^{-1}$$

❑ **on descending a group in the Periodic Table the first ionisation energy decreases**

❑ the electron to be removed from the outer energy level is increasingly distant from the nucleus as a result of the increasing size of the atom;
the attraction of the positive nucleus for that electron diminishes and it therefore becomes easier to pull it away

❑ electrons in the inner energy levels will shield (or screen) those in the outer energy level from the full nuclear charge and so lessen the attraction between the nucleus and the electron to be removed;
as the number of inner electrons increases, the shielding effect will increase and consequently it will become easier to remove an outer electron

❑ **on crossing a period in the Periodic Table, from left to right, there is a general increase in first ionisation energy**

❑ protons are being added to the nucleus and so the electrons will experience an increasing nuclear charge; the electron to be removed from the outermost energy level will therefore be held more tightly and so it will become more difficult to remove it

❑ the atomic size decreases; this decreasing distance between the electron to be removed and the nucleus will increase the attraction of the nucleus for that electron; more energy therefore will be required to remove it

❑ more than one electron can be removed from an atom and so, in addition to the first ionisation energy, there can also be second, third and fourth etc. ionisation energies of an element,

e.g. the second ionisation energy of magnesium

$$Mg^+_{(g)} \rightarrow Mg^{2+}_{(g)} + e^- \quad \Delta H = +1460 \text{ kJ mol}^{-1}$$

e.g. the third ionisation energy of aluminium

$$Al^{2+}_{(g)} \rightarrow Al^{3+}_{(g)} + e^- \quad \Delta H = +2760 \text{ kJ mol}^{-1}$$

❑ ionisation energy is also an example of a periodic property

❑ the ionisation energies of selected elements are found on page 10 of the Data Booklet

(c) Electronegativity

❏ atoms of different elements have different attractions for bonding electrons

increasing electronegativity →

❏ electronegativity is the measure of attraction an atom involved in a bond has for the electrons in the bond

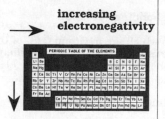

❏ electronegativity is also an example of a periodic property

decreasing electronegativity

❏ the electronegativity values increase from left to right across a period in the Periodic Table and decrease down a group

❏ the electronegativities of selected elements are found on page 10 of the Data Booklet

4. BONDING, STRUCTURE AND PROPERTIES

Covalent and ionic bonding - revision

❑ the noble gases which are in Group 0 (8) of the Periodic Table are made up of atoms which have filled outer energy levels (shells); this is a very stable electron arrangement

(a) Ionic bonding

❑ metals usually react with non-metals to form ionic compounds; the metal atoms lose electrons to achieve the stable electron arrangement of a noble gas thus forming metal ions with a positive charge; the non-metal atoms gain electrons to achieve the stable electron arrangement of a noble gas thus forming non-metal ions with a negative charge; the force of attraction between oppositely charged ions is known as an **ionic bond**

(b) Covalent bonding

❑ when two non-metals join to make a compound, the stable electron arrangement of a noble gas is achieved by atoms sharing electrons; this overlap of half-filled electron clouds is known as **covalent bonding**; a group of atoms held together in this way is called a **molecule**

❑ the shapes of molecules are based on a tetrahedron,

e.g.

methane

ammonia

Covalent and ionic bonding - energy considerations

(a) Covalent bonding

❑ the protons give a positive charge to the nucleus of the atoms; the electrons give a negative charge to the part of the atom surrounding the nucleus; the merging or overlapping of half-filled clouds to form the covalent bond increases the negative charge in the overlap region; the positive nuclei of both atoms attract the electrons in the overlap region and this holds the atoms together

+ve nucleus   **+ve nucleus**
●   ●

**-ve charge
due to electrons**

⟷   ⟷
attraction   attraction

❑ the forces of attraction result in an overall decrease in potential energy

❑ a lot of energy is required to overcome the forces of attraction; covalent bonds are therefore strong (100 to 500 kJ mol^{-1})

(b) Ionic bonding

❑ ionic bonding is the force of atraction between oppositely charged ions,

e.g. in the formation of sodium chloride

$$Na^+(g) \quad + \quad Cl^-(g) \quad \rightarrow \quad NaCl(s)$$

❑ large amounts of energy are required to overcome the forces of attraction between oppositely charged ions; ionic bonds are therefore strong (100 to 450 kJ mol^{-1})

Bonding in compounds

❑ pure covalent bonding is only found in elements, i.e. when the bonded atoms are identical so that the bonding electrons are shared equally between the atoms,

e.g. H$_2$, Cl$_2$, etc.

❑ in most covalent compounds the bonding is **polar covalent**, i.e. the bonding electrons are not equally shared but are pulled closer to one of the atoms

❑ polar covalent compounds arise when the difference in the electronegativity values is not so great as to lead to typically ionic bonding

❑ the atom with the higher electronegativity will have a slight negative charge compared to the other atom,

e.g. chlorine has a higher electronegativity than hydrogen so hydrogen chloride can be represented

$$\overset{\delta+}{H} - \overset{\delta-}{Cl}$$

δ the Greek letter 'd' means 'very small'

❑ there is therefore a small permanent positive charge on the hydrogen atoms and a small permanent negative charge on the chlorine atoms

❑ there are also polar covalent bonds in water

$$\overset{\delta-}{O}$$
$$\overset{\delta+}{H} \qquad H\overset{\delta+}{}$$

❑ carbon and hydrogen atoms have almost the same electronegativity so hydrocarbons have almost non-polar covalent bonds

- the classification of bonds into covalent and ionic is an over-simplification; pure covalent and ionic compounds are opposite ends of a continuum and the bonding in most compounds is intermediate in character

- the type of conding in a compound is related to the position of its constituent elements in the Periodic Table

- the greater the difference in electronegativity values, the greater the ionic character of the bonds formed

- since metals tend to have low electronegativity values and non-metals tend to have high electronegativity values, metals and non-metals combine to form ionic bonds,

   e.g. *typical ionic compounds are sodium chloride, Na^+Cl^- and magnesium oxide $Mg^{2+}O^{2-}$*

- because of the difference in electronegativity values, hydrogen can react with metals to form ionic compounds containing the hydride ion, H^-,

   e.g. *sodium hydride, Na^+H^- and magnesium hydride, $Mg^{2+}(H^-)_2$*

Metallic bonding

- atoms in a metal contribute the electrons in their outermost energy levels to a common 'pool' of free or delocalised electrons

- each positively charged ion is attracted to the pool of negative electrons and vice versa; these electrostatic attractions constitute the metallic bonds

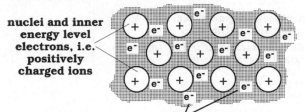

nuclei and inner energy level electrons, i.e. positively charged ions

delocalised outer energy level electrons

- a lot of energy is required to overcome the forces of attraction; as a result, metallic bonds are strong ($80 - 600$ kJ mol^{-1})

- the greater the number of delocalised electrons and consequently the greater the charge on the ions, the stronger will be the metallic bond,
   e.g. *Group 1 metals have weaker metallic bonds than the corresponding Group 2 metals*

Intermolecular forces

❏ **intermolecular forces** are forces of attraction between different molecules

(a) Van der Waals' forces

❏ **van der Waals' forces** are the weak intermolecular forces of attraction in discrete non-polar molecules and the Group O elements when they are in the solid or liquid states

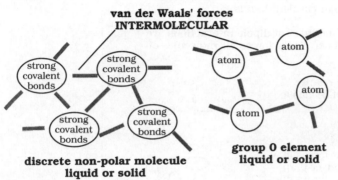

since electrons are constantly moving, at any particular moment in time the electron distribution within the molecule (or atom) is unlikely to be evenly spread; momentarily there may be more negative charge on one side of the molecule (or atom) than on the other; this unequal distribution of charge is called a dipole; the van der Waals' forces are a result of electrostatic attractions between the temporary and induced dipoles

❏ van der Waals' forces have to be overcome before the discrete molecular elements melt or boil;

since they are weak (approximately 4 kJ mol^{-1}) these elements are either gases, liquids or low melting point solids at room temperature

❏ the strength of the van der Waals' forces increases with increasing molecular mass,

e.g. the boiling point of the halogens increases going down Group 7 of the Periodic Table

❏ for a fair comparison of the strengths of different types of intermolecular forces the molecular masses should therefore be approximately the same

(b) Permanent dipole-permanent dipole attractions

❏ a permanent dipole is due to a difference in electronegativity between the atoms involved in a covalent bond,

e.g.

$$\overset{\delta^-}{O}$$
$$\underset{\delta^+H}{\diagup}\quad\underset{H\delta^+}{\diagdown}$$

$$\overset{\delta^+\ \ \delta^-}{H-Cl}$$

❏ permanent dipole-permanent dipole interactions are additional electrostatic forces of attraction between molecules with polar covalent bonds

❏ permanent dipole-permanent dipole interactions are stronger than van der Waals' forces for molecules of equivalent mass

❏ propanone with a relative molecular mass of 58 has a polar bond

$$CH_3-\underset{\delta+}{\overset{\overset{\displaystyle O}{\parallel}}{C}}-CH_3 \quad \overset{\delta-}{}$$

❏ the intermolecular forces in the liquid are stronger than the van der Waals' forces due to the permanent dipole-permanent dipole attractions

associated with the $\overset{\delta+}{\diagdown}C=O\overset{\delta-}{}$ bond

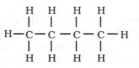

permanent dipole-permanent dipole attractions

❏ butane also with a relative molecular mass of 58 does not have polar bonds

$$\underset{\underset{H\ \ \ H\ \ \ H\ \ \ H}{|\ \ \ \ |\ \ \ \ |\ \ \ \ |}}{\overset{\overset{H\ \ \ H\ \ \ H\ \ \ H}{|\ \ \ \ |\ \ \ \ |\ \ \ \ |}}{H-C-C-C-C-H}}$$

❏ the intermolecular forces in liquid butane are weaker than in propanone

van der Waals' forces

❏ the stronger intermolecular forces are responsible for the relatively high boiling point of propanone (56°C) compared with butane (0°C)

❏ the boiling points of propanone and butane can be used to compare the strengths of the intermolecular forces between molecules containing polar bonds with the normal van der Waals' forces **because these compounds have the same relative molecular mass**

(c) Hydrogen bonding

❑ for a non-metal, hydrogen has a very low electronegativity; molecules which contain a hydrogen atom bonded to a small atom with a high electronegativity, i.e. fluorine, nitrogen or oxygen, will therefore be highly polar covalent

$$\overset{\delta+}{H}-\overset{\delta-}{F} \qquad \overset{\delta+}{H}\underset{\underset{H}{\delta+}}{\overset{\overset{\delta-}{N}}{|}}H^{\delta+} \qquad \overset{\delta+}{H}\overset{\overset{\delta-}{O}}{}\overset{\delta+}{H}$$

❑ the relatively strong intermolecular forces (approximately 30 kJ mol^{-1}) in such molecules are known as **hydrogen bonds**

❑ a hydrogen bond is stronger than other intermolecular forces but weaker than a covalent bond

❑ the boiling points of the Group 4 hydrides decrease from stannane (SnH$_4$) to methane (CH$_4$);
this decrease is an expected one in view of the fact that the molecular mass is decreasing

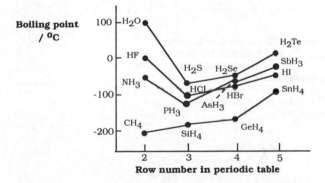

❑ there is a similar and expected decrease in boiling point from hydrogen telluride (H$_2$Te) though hydrogen selenide (H$_2$Se) to hydrogen sulphide (H$_2$S) but water has a much higher boiling point than might have been anticipated

❑ a similar pattern emerges with the hydrides of the Group 5 and Group 7 elements where the boiling points for ammonia (NH$_3$) and hydrogen fluoride (HF) are much higher than extrapolation of the plots would suggest

❑ hydrogen bonding in water, liquid ammonia and liquid hydrogen fluoride account for their unexpected high boiling points

❑ considerable energy is required to overcome the relatively strong intermolecular forces

- in hydrogen fluoride the relatively strong forces of attraction between the hydrogen atoms and the fluorine atoms of neighbouring molecules in the liquid and solid states results in long hydrogen bonded chains

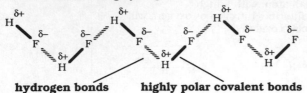

hydrogen bonds   **highly polar covalent bonds**

- the density of water increases as the temperature falls to $4^\circ C$ but from $4^\circ C$ to $0^\circ C$ the density decreases with the formation of ice; the water molecules begin to move further apart to form an open and rigid structure held together by hydrogen bonds

- the fact that ice is less dense than water means that ponds and rivers will freeze from the surface downwards and the layer of ice insulates the water below, thus preventing complete solidification and allowing plant-life and fish-life to continue

Polar molecules

- although differences in attractions for the bonding electrons allow the polarity of a **bond** to be predicted, it is necessary to look at the symmetry of a molecule before predicting whether a **molecule** is polar

- in polar molecules, the polar bonds are **not** arranged symmetrically in the molecule,

    e.g.

- in non-polar molecules there is a symmetrical arrangement of polar bonds and the permanent dipole-permanent dipole attractions cancel out,

    e.g.

- there is a difference in behaviour between polar and non-polar molecules in an electric field;
  polar molecules are attracted by the electric field
  non-polar molecules are unaffected

Structure and properties - the first twenty elements

❑ differences in electrical conductivity and melting points enable the elements to be grouped according to bonding and structure

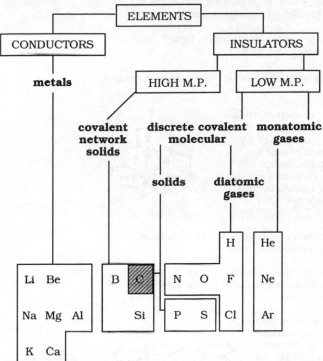

(a) Metals

❑ a metallic structure consists of a giant lattice of positively charged ions in a sea of delocalised outer electrons

❑ the outer electrons which are contributed to the pool are free to move from one ion to another throughout the metal lattice

❑ the metallic bonds hold the entire metal lattice together as a single unit

(b) Covalent network solids

❏ a covalent network structure consists of a giant lattice of covalently bonded atoms

❏ these elements have very high melting points because melting involves breaking of covalent bonds

❏ boron has a covalent network structure based on interlocking B_{12} molecular units

❏ carbon exists in two different crystalline forms, diamond and graphite

❏ in diamond, each carbon atom is at the centre of a regular tetrahedron and surrounded by four other carbon atoms at the corners of the tetrahedron; each atom forms four covalent bonds by sharing electrons with each of its four nearest neighbours

❏ since all the electrons are localised in the covalent bonds, diamond does not conduct electricity

❏ the rigid three dimensional structure with its strong covalent bonds makes diamond very hard and it is used for cutting

❏ in graphite, each carbon atom forms covalent bonds with three neighbouring atoms; the carbon atoms join to make up a planar arrangement of hexagonal plates which are held together by weak forces of attraction and so easily slip over each other

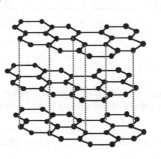

❏ graphite can be used as a lubricant and as 'lead' in pencils

❏ since only three electrons from each carbon atom are localised through covalent bonding, the fourth electron is free to move, making graphite a conductor of electricity

❏ silicon has a similar crystal structure to diamond but whereas diamond is a non-conductor of electricity silicon is a semi-conductor

(c) Discrete covalent molecular solids and gases

❏ a covalent molecular structure consists of discrete molecules held together by weak intermolecular forces

❏ phosphorus and sulphur are solids at room temperature due to their higher molecular masses

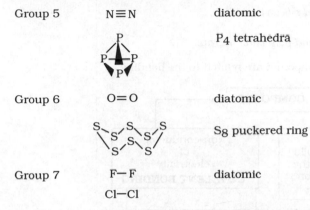

Group 5	$N \equiv N$	diatomic
		P_4 tetrahedra
Group 6	$O = O$	diatomic
		S_8 puckered ring
Group 7	$F - F$	diatomic
	$Cl - Cl$	

❏ it is the weak intermolecular forces (van der Waals' forces) which account for the typically low melting and boiling points

❏ carbon exists as covalent molecules in **fullerenes**; the first molecule to be discovered consists of 60 carbon atoms, C_{60}; the pattern of the structure is spherical, the same as a football albeit considerably smaller

(d) Monatomic gases

❏ elements have low melting and boiling points due to the weak intermolecular forces

❏ each of the noble gases consists of atoms with filled outer energy levels and accordingly the atoms are relatively unreactive

Structure and properties - compounds

❏ compounds each adopt one of three structures in the solid state:
discrete covalent molecular,
e.g. carbon dioxide and methane
covalent network,
e.g. silicon dioxide and silicon carbide
ionic,
e.g. sodium chloride and potassium nitrate

❏ the properties of a compound are related to the bonding and structure

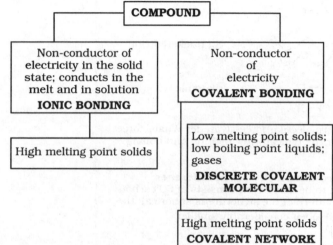

(a) Ionic compounds

❏ an ionic structure consists of a giant lattice of oppositely charged ions

❏ ionic compounds have high melting points;
all ionic compounds are solid at room temperature;
this is because there are very strong forces of attraction holding together the oppositely charged ions

❏ ionic compounds do not conduct electricity in the solid state because the ions are not free to move;
ionic compounds do conduct when in the liquid state or when dissolved in water; the decomposition of a melt or a solution by the movement of ions is called **electrolysis**

(b) Covalent discrete molecular compounds

❑ covalent discrete molecular compounds do **not** conduct electricity

❑ compounds which are gases or liquids at room temperature have low melting and boiling points; such compounds are made up of covalent molecules; whereas the covalent bonds holding together the atoms in a molecule are strong, the van der Waals' forces between different molecules are relatively weak

❑ discrete molecular covalent compounds can also be solid at room temperature; such compounds are made up of larger molecules with a higher molecular mass

(c) Covalent network compounds

❑ covalent network compounds do **not** conduct electricity

❑ some covalent compounds have network structures, i.e. they consist of giant molecules,
  e.g. silicon dioxide and silicon carbide

❑ these compounds have very high melting points compared with the discrete molecular compounds because melting compounds with network structures involves the actual breaking of covalent bonds

❑ both compounds are very hard due to the network of strong covalent bonds

❑ silicon dioxide is found as quartz; each silicon atom in silicon dioxide is bonded to four oxygen atoms to give SiO_4 tetrahedra; these are linked using the oxygen atoms as bridges

❑ silicon carbide is found as carborundum; it is used as an abrasive in the cutting and grinding of the surfaces of tools

Solubility

❑ many ionic compounds are soluble in water and this is a result of the polar nature of the water molecules

❑ the slight negative ends of the polar water molecules are attracted to the positive ions in the crystal lattice while the slight positive ends of the water molecules are attracted to the negative ions

❑ the formation of electrostatic attractions between the ions and the water molecules results in a release of energy

❑ this energy is used to overcome the electrostatic attractions between the oppositely charged ions in the lattice

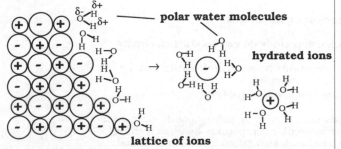

polar water molecules

hydrated ions

lattice of ions

❑ polar molecular compounds can also be soluble in water, *e.g. hydrogen chloride*

❑ sufficient energy is released by the electrostatic attractions between the hydrogen chloride molecules and water molecules to overcome the forces of attraction

❑ while ionic (and polar molecular) compounds will often dissolve in polar solvents, like water and ethanol, they are less likely to be soluble in non-polar solvents, like tetrachloromethane and benzene

❑ interactions between the ions (and polar molecules) and the non-polar solvent molecules would be so weak that insufficient energy would be released to overcome the ionic bonds (and forces of attraction between polar molecules)

❑ generally, non-polar substances dissolve in non-polar solvents but are insoluble in polar solvents,

   e.g. iodine is soluble in tetrachloromethane but does not dissolve in water

❑ little energy is required to overcome the weak van der Waals' forces between the tetrachloromethane molecules in the solvent and sufficient energy is released to do this when iodine molecules set up van der Waals' forces with tetrachloromethane molecules

- insufficient energy would be released in setting up van der Waals' forces between iodine molecules and water molecules in order to overcome the stronger hydrogen bonds between the water molecules

Ionisation in water

- hydrogen chloride is a covalent gas at room temperature, $HCl(g)$; $$\overset{\delta+\quad\delta-}{H-Cl}$$ the bonds in hydrogen chloride are highly polar covalent

- when hydrogen chloride reacts with water, energy is released when the attractions are set up between the hydrogen chloride molecules and the polar water molecules; this energy is more than sufficient to break the covalent bonds in all the hydrogen chloride molecules

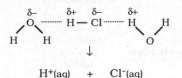

$$H^+(aq) \quad + \quad Cl^-(aq)$$

- hydrogen chloride therefore completely ionises in water to form an acidic solution

- this explains why an aqueous solution of hydrogen chloride, $HCl(aq)$, is a good conductor of electricity

- other polar covalent substances completely ionise in water to form acidic solutions,

  e.g. the other hydrogen halides $HF(g)$, $HBr(g)$, $HI(g)$ and pure concentrated sulphuric acid, $H_2SO_4(l)$

5. THE MOLE

The Avogadro Constant

❑ one mole of any substance contains the same number of 'elementary entities' as there are atoms in exactly 12 g of carbon-12

❑ elementary entities may be atoms, molecules, ions, electrons or other particles

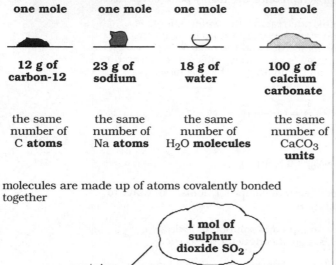

one mole	**one mole**	**one mole**	**one mole**
12 g of carbon-12	**23 g of sodium**	**18 g of water**	**100 g of calcium carbonate**
the same number of C **atoms**	the same number of Na **atoms**	the same number of H_2O **molecules**	the same number of $CaCO_3$ **units**

❑ molecules are made up of atoms covalently bonded together

1 mol of sulphur dioxide SO_2

contains

1 mol of molecules

but →

1 mol of sulphur atoms

2 mol of oxygen atoms

3 mol of atoms altogether

❑ ionic compounds are made up of oppositely charged ions held together by forces of attraction

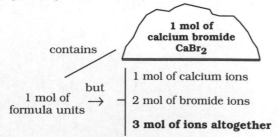

1 mol of calcium bromide $CaBr_2$

contains

1 mol of formula units

but →

1 mol of calcium ions

2 mol of bromide ions

3 mol of ions altogether

❑ the actual number of elementary entities per mole is known as the **Avogadro Constant**, (symbol L)

- the Avogadro Constant = 6.02×10^{23} mol^{-1}

- for elements with a formula which is just the chemical symbol, the chemical units are atoms,

  e.g. 1 mol of copper, Cu, contains 6.02×10^{23} Cu atoms,

     0.5 mol of argon, Ar, contains 3.01×10^{23} Ar atoms

- for covalently bonded elements and compounds the chemical units are molecules,

  e.g. 1 mol of water, H_2O,
                   contains 6.02×10^{23} H_2O molecules,

     0.1 mol of methane, CH_4,
                   contains 6.02×10^{22} CH_4 molecules

- for ionic compounds the chemical units are formula units,

  e.g. 1 mol of magnesium chloride, $MgCl_2$,
                  contains 6.02×10^{23} $MgCl_2$ formula units,

     2 mol of sodium sulphate, Na_2SO_4,
                  contains 1.204×10^{24} Na_2SO_4 formula units

Example 1

Which contains more atoms, 6 g of carbon or 6 g of sodium?

1 mol of carbon   =   12 g

1 mol of sodium   =   23 g

6 g of carbon has a greater number of moles and hence contains more atoms.

Example 2

Which contains more molecules, 36 g of water or 44 g of carbon dioxide?

1 mol of water (H_2O) ⟷   18 g

2 mol   ⟷   36 g

1 mol of carbon dioxide (CO_2)   =   44 g

36 g of water has a greater number of moles and hence contains more molecules.

Example 3

Which contains more ions, 6.2 g of sodium oxide or 10.11 g of potasium nitrate?

1 mol of sodium oxide (Na_2O) ⟷ 62 g

0.1 mol ⟷ 6.2 g

Each Na_2O unit contains three ions, i.e. two Na^+ and one O^{2-}

1 mol of potassium nitrate (KNO_3) ⟷ 101.1 g

0.1 mol ⟷ 10.11 g

Each KNO_3 unit contains two ions, i.e. one K^+ and one NO_3^-

0.1 mol of Na_2O contains 0.3 mol of ions, whereas 0.1 mol of KNO_3 contains 0.2 mol of ions.

Example 4

How many atoms are in 0.6 g of carbon?

1 mol of carbon   = 12 g

12 g (1 mol) ⟷ 6×10^{23} atoms

0.6 g ⟷ $6 \times 10^{23} \times \dfrac{0.6}{12}$

= **3×10^{22} atoms**

Example 5

How many molecules in 3.2×10^{-3} g methane?

1 mol of methane (CH_4)   = 16 g

16 g (1 mol) ⟷ 6×10^{23} molecules

3.2×10^{-3} g ⟷ $6 \times 10^{23} \times \dfrac{3.2 \times 10^{-3}}{16}$

= **1.2×10^{20} molecules**

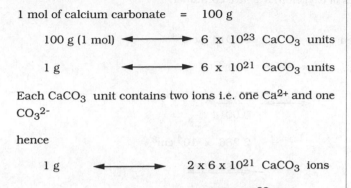

Example 6

How many ions in 1g of calcium carbonate?

1 mol of calcium carbonate = 100 g

100 g (1 mol) $\longleftrightarrow$ 6×10^{23} $CaCO_3$ units

1 g $\longleftrightarrow$ 6×10^{21} $CaCO_3$ units

Each $CaCO_3$ unit contains two ions i.e. one Ca^{2+} and one CO_3^{2-}

hence

1 g $\longleftrightarrow$ $2 \times 6 \times 10^{21}$ $CaCO_3$ ions

= **1.2×10^{22} ions**

Molar volume of gases

❏ the molar volume of a gas is the volume occupied by one mole (at a certain temperature and pressure)

Example 1

The volume of 3.4 g of ammonia is 4.5 litres.
Calculate the volume of 1 mol of ammonia at the same temperature and pressure.

17 g ammonia (NH_3) $\longleftrightarrow$ 1 mol

3.4 g $\longleftrightarrow$ 0.2 mol

0.2 mol $\longleftrightarrow$ 4.5 litres

1 mol $\longleftrightarrow$ **22.5 litres**

Example 2

Using the density given in the Data Booklet, calculate the volume of 10 mol of hydrogen.

density of hydrogen = 9×10^{-5} g cm^{-3}

9×10^{-5} g $\longleftrightarrow$ 1 cm^3

2g (1 mol) $\longleftrightarrow$ $\dfrac{2}{9 \times 10^{-5}} \times 1$

$= 2.222 \times 10^4$ cm^3

$= $ 22.22 litres

1 mol $\longleftrightarrow$ 22.22 litres

10 mol $\longleftrightarrow$ **222.2 litres**

Example 3

Using the density given in the Data Booklet, calculate the number of moles of oxygen in a 2 litre container.

density of oxygen $\qquad$ = $\qquad$ 0.0014 g cm^{-3}

0.0014 g $\longleftrightarrow$ 1 cm^3

32 g (1 mol) $\longleftrightarrow$ $\dfrac{32}{0.0014}$ x 1

$\qquad\qquad\qquad\qquad$ = $\qquad$ 2.286 x 10^4 cm^3

$\qquad\qquad\qquad\qquad$ = $\qquad$ <u>22.86 litres</u>

22.86 litres $\longleftrightarrow$ 1 mol

2 litres $\longleftrightarrow$ $\dfrac{2}{22.86}$ x 1

$\qquad\qquad\qquad\qquad$ = $\qquad$ **0.087 mol**

❑ when doing experiments with gases it is much more convenient to measure volumes than masses

Example 1

Calculate the volume of hydrogen produced when 0.2 g of zinc reacts with excess dilute sulphuric acid.

(Take the molar volume of hydrogen to be 22.2 litres mol^{-1}.)

balanced equation

$\qquad$ Zn $\quad$ + $\quad$ H$_2$SO$_{4(aq)}$ $\quad \rightarrow \quad$ ZnSO$_4$ $\quad$ + $\quad$ H$_2$

$\qquad$ 1 mol $\qquad\qquad\qquad\qquad\qquad$ 1 mol

$\qquad$ 65.4 g $\quad\longleftrightarrow\quad$ 22.2 litres

$\qquad$ 0.2 g $\quad\longleftrightarrow\quad$ $\dfrac{0.2 \times 22.2}{65.4}$

$\qquad\qquad\qquad\qquad$ = $\qquad$ **67.9 cm^3**

Example 2

Calculate the volume of carbon dioxide produced by the complete combustion of 7 g of ethene, C_2H_4.

(Take the molar volume of carbon dioxide to be 22.0 litres mol^{-1}.)

balanced equation

$$C_2H_4 \quad + \quad 3O_2 \quad \rightarrow \quad 2CO_2 \quad + \quad 2H_2O$$

1 mol   2 mol

28 g (1 mol) ⟷   2 x 22 litres

7 g ⟷ $\dfrac{7 \times 2 \times 22}{28}$

= **11 litres**

Calculations involving volumes

❑ one mole of any gas contains the same number of molecules (or atoms in the case of the noble gases) and occupies the same volume (at the same temperature and pressure)

❑ this means that equal volumes of gases contain the same number of moles

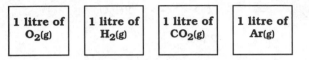

| 1 litre of $O_2(g)$ | 1 litre of $H_2(g)$ | 1 litre of $CO_2(g)$ | 1 litre of $Ar(g)$ |

same number of moles

❑ the balanced equation gives the relative number of moles of reactants and products,

e.g. $N_2(g)$ + $3H_2(g)$ → $2NH_3(g)$

　　　　1 mol　　　3 mol　　　　　　　2 mol

hence...
　　　1 litre　+　3 litre　　→　　2 litre

or... 10 cm³　+　30 cm³　　→　　20 cm³

or... 1 cm³　+　3 cm³　　→　　2 cm³

❑ in the above reaction the volume of the product is half the volume of the reactants

❑ liquid or solid reactants and products have negligible volume,

e.g.　　　$C(s)$　+　$O_2(g)$　→　$CO_2(g)$

　　　　　1 mol　　1 mol　　　1 mol

hence...　not a gas　1 litre　→　1 litre

or...　　　　　　　　10 cm³　→　10 cm³

or...　　　　　　　　1 cm³　→　1 cm³

❑ in this reaction the volume of the product is equal to the volume of the reactant

Example 1

What volume of oxygen is required for 50 cm^3 of hydrogen to completely burn to produce water?

balanced equation $2H_{2(g)}$ + $O_{2(g)} \rightarrow$ $2H_2O_{(l)}$

                    2 mol   1 mol

so...   50cm^3 +   **25cm^3**

Example 2

30 cm^3 of methane is completely burned in 100 cm^3 of oxygen.
What is the volume and composition of the gas at the end of the experiment at 20 °C?

balanced equation CH_4 + $2O_2 \rightarrow CO_2$ + $2H_2O$

                        1 mol   2 mol   1 mol   2 mol

Which reactant is in excess?

From the balanced equation,

    1 mol of CH_4 reacts with 2 mol of O_2

    30 cm^3 of CH_4 reacts with 60 cm^3 of O_2

Since there is 100 cm^3 of O_2, O_2 is in excess.

Which reactant controls the volume of products?

Oxygen is in excess; the methane will all be used up; the volume of products will depend on the volume of methane.

Complete calculation

        CH_4 + $2O_2 \rightarrow$ CO_2 + $2H_2O$

        1 mol   2 mol   1 mol   2 mol

        30 cm^3 60 cm^3 30 cm^3 (not a gas)

        Volumes which react   Volumes which are
                                    produced

    Volumes of gases at the end of experiment

            O_2 (unreacted)   100 cm^3 - 60 cm^3 = **40 cm^3**
            CO_2 (produced)   **30 cm^3**

Unit 2   The World of Carbon

1. FUELS

Obtaining petrol - revision

❑ carbon compounds are often referred to as **organic** compounds and the study of the chemistry of carbon compounds is often called **organic chemistry**; this is because many of the wide variety of carbon compounds originate from living organisms,
e.g. the fuels and consumer products from crude oil

❑ a chemical which is burned to provide energy is called a **fuel**

❑ crude oil is a complex mixture of different hydrocarbons which have different boiling points due to the different molecular structures

❑ the different hydrocarbons are separated according to their boiling points by **fractional distillation** into **fractions**,
e.g. petroleum gases, petrol, kerosine, gas oil, residue

❑ the largest molecules are found in the fraction with the highest boiling points; this is because the van der Waals' forces between different molecules become stronger with increasing molecular size

❑ the typical range of carbon atoms in molecules found in petrol is from C_4 to C_{12}

Ignition

❑ in a petrol engine, a mixture of petrol vapour and air is ignited by a spark in a cylinder

❑ the more volatile hydrocarbons vaporise more readily; any petrol is a blend (mix) of hydrocarbons of different volatilities which takes account of prevailing temperatures

❑ for colder temperatures, more volatile components are used so that the petrol vaporises more easily; this means adding more hydrocarbons with small molecules, like butane and pentane, to the blend; the blend for warmer temperatures contains more hydrocarbons with larger molecules so that the petrol does not vaporise so easily

Auto-ignition

❑ the petrol-air mixture in a petrol engine is compressed in a cylinder before it is ignited; as the mixture is compressed it becomes hotter

- auto-ignition occurs when the compression of the mixture causes an explosion before it is sparked; auto-ignition, which produces a sound in the engine commonly known as 'knocking', lowers engine performance and can damage the inside of the cylinders

- the addition of lead compounds reduces the tendency of the hydrocarbons in petrol to auto-ignite; however, concern about environmental effects and also the poisoning of the metal catalysts in catalytic convertors has led to the use of unleaded petrol

Improving the blends

- in order to ensure smooth burning in high performance engines unleaded petrol requires the use of branched-chain alkanes, cycloalkanes and aromatics, as well as straight-chain alkanes

- the petrol fraction which is produced by the distillation of crude oil contains no aromatics or cycloalkanes and insufficient branched-chain alkanes; these components of petrol are produced by the **reforming** of naphtha

- reforming is a set of processes each of which alters the arrangement of atoms in molecules without necessarily changing the size of the molecules,
  e.g.

$$CH_3\text{-}CH_2\text{-}CH_2\text{-}CH_2\text{-}CH_2\text{-}CH_2\text{-}CH_3 \rightarrow$$

$$CH_3\text{-}\underset{\underset{CH_3}{|}}{\overset{\overset{CH_3}{|}}{C}}\text{-}CH_2\text{-}CH_2\text{-}CH_3$$

heptane

2,2-dimethylpentane
(a branched-chain alkane)

$$CH_3\text{-}CH_2\text{-}CH_2\text{-}CH_2\text{-}CH_2\text{-}CH_3 \rightarrow$$

cyclohexane structure $+ H_2$

hexane

cyclohexane
(a cycloalkane)

 $\rightarrow$ benzene structure $+ 3H_2$

cyclohexane

benzene
(an aromatic hydrocarbon)

Pollution problems

❏ in a limited supply of air, the hydrocarbons in fuels burn to produce carbon monoxide - a very poisonous gas

❏ in a car engine, the gases of the air react to produce oxides of nitrogen; the gases react because there is sufficient energy associated with the spark from the plugs; these oxides dissolve in water to produce acidic solutions

❏ one way to reduce carbon monoxide and oxides of nitrogen is to fit car exhaust systems with a catalytic converter

❏ compounds of lead are added to some petrols to help the petrol to burn more smoothly; these compounds are poisonous and pass out with the exhaust gases; cars with catalytic converters take lead-free petrol to prevent poisoning of the catalyst

❏ many fossil fuels contain sulphur compounds which burn to produce sulphur dioxide gas; this gas is very soluble in water and is one of the main causes of acid rain

❏ when fossil fuels burn in a plentiful supply of air, the carbon in the compounds forms carbon dioxide gas; the increased use of fossil fuels has led to increased concentrations of the gas in the air; also, the cutting down of large forests has meant that less carbon dioxide is being removed from the air by plants during photosynthesis; the build-up of carbon dioxide may be contributing to the gradual heating up of the Earth - **global warming**

Renewable sources of energy

❏ one of the main disadvantages of fossil fuels is that they are finite sources of energy; this means that supplies of petrol are not renewable

❏ ethanol is a fuel which can be obtained by the fermentation of sugar cane which can be considered as a renewable source of energy; as a result, ethanol is being mixed with petrol for use as an engine fuel in countries where it can be economically produced in sufficient quantities,
e.g. in Brazil

❏ some biological matter, like plant and animal materials, decays under anaerobic conditions, i.e. in the absence of air; this process is called **anaerobic respiration** or incomplete **fermentation**

❏ a gaseous mixture is produced which consists mainly of methane; this can be used as a fuel

❏   in rural areas, increasing quantities of methane are being produced from manure and straw

Methanol

❏   there are both advantages and disadvantages of using methanol as an alternative fuel to petrol

Advantages
*   combustion is more complete, and so carbon monoxide emissions are reduced
*   benzene vapour or other aromatic hydrocarbons (which are carcinogenic) are not released into the air
*   relatively cheap
*   less volatile and so less likely to explode in a car collision

Disadvantages
*   toxic; long term exposure can cause blindness and brain damage
*   for an equal volume, methanol produces less energy than petrol
*   absorbs water to produce a corrosive mixture
*   it is difficult to get methanol to mix with petrol

The hydrogen economy

❏   in the future, a 'hydrogen economy' could see the use of hydrogen as a major source of energy

❏   hydrogen could be used to produce electricity in a hydrogen/oxygen fuel cell, for burning as a heating fuel or as a fuel in internal combustion engines

❏   the use of hydrogen in the internal combustion engine would reduce the build up of carbon dioxide in the atmosphere

❏   hydrogen could be stored and distributed like natural gas; over a period of time this could be cheaper than using electricity

❏   a 'hydrogen economy' would only be cost-effective if the hydrogen is obtained without using fossil fuels to produce electricity

❏   the most likely large-scale method would appear to be by electrolysis of water using solar energy

❏   the ideal long-term solution would be to use solar energy to decompose water to produce hydrogen using routes which absorb light energy from the Sun

2. NOMENCLATURE AND STRUCTURAL FORMULAE

Alkanes, alkenes and cycloalkanes - revision

❑ the **alkanes** are a subset of the set of hydrocarbons

❑ each member of the alkane series has a name which ends in **-ane** and a prefix which indicates the number of carbon atoms in the molecule

Prefix	Number of C atoms	Prefix	Number of C atoms
meth-	1	pent-	5
eth-	2	hex-	6
prop-	3	hept-	7
but-	4	oct-	8

❑ the general formula for the alkanes is C_nH_{2n+2} where n is the number of carbon atoms

❑ the **full structural formula** can be used to show the arrangement of atoms;
a **shortened structural** formula can be used to show the grouping of hydrogen atoms round each carbon,

e.g.

Number of carbon atoms in each molecule	Name of alkane	Formula
4	butane	C_4H_{10}

Full structural formula	Shortened structural formula

H H H H
   | | | |
 H–C–C–C–C–H
   | | | |
 H H H H
	$CH_3\text{-}CH_2\text{-}CH_2\text{-}CH_3$
	 or
	 $CH_3CH_2CH_2CH_3$

❑ all alkanes are **saturated** hydrocarbons, i.e. all the carbon to carbon bonds are single covalent bonds

❑ the **alkenes** are also a subset of the set of hydrocarbons

❑ each member of the alkene series has a name which ends in **-ene** and a prefix which indicates the number of carbon atoms in the molecule

- the general formula for the alkenes is C_nH_{2n} (each alkene has two hydrogens less than the corresponding alkane due to the double bond),

e.g.

Number of carbon atoms in each molecule	Name of alkene	Formula
3	propene	C_3H_6

Full structural formula	Shortened structural formula
$\begin{array}{c} H \quad\quad H \\ \diagdown \quad\quad \vert \\ C{=}C{-}C{-}H \\ \diagup \quad \vert \;\; \vert \\ H \quad H \; H \end{array}$	$CH_2{=}CH{-}CH_3$ or CH_2CHCH_3

- all alkenes are **unsaturated** hydrocarbons, i.e. there is at least one carbon to carbon double bond

- the carbon to carbon double bond is an example of a **functional group**, i.e. a group of atoms with characteristic properties

- alkanes with a ring of carbon atoms are called **cycloalkanes**

- the general formula for the cycloalkanes is also C_nH_{2n} (each cycloalkane has two hydrogens less than the corresponding alkane due to the closing of the chain),

e.g.

Number of carbon atoms in each molecule	Name of cycloalkane	Formula
6	cyclohexane	C_6H_{12}

Full structural formula	Shortened structural formula
$\begin{array}{c} H \;\; H \\ \diagdown\;\diagup \\ H\diagdown \;\; C \;\; \diagup H \\ H{-}C \quad C{-}H \\ \vert \quad\quad \vert \\ H{-}C \quad C{-}H \\ H\diagup \;\; C \;\; \diagdown H \\ \diagup\;\diagdown \\ H \;\; H \end{array}$	$\begin{array}{c} CH_2 \\ \diagup \quad \diagdown \\ CH_2 \;\; CH_2 \\ \vert \quad\quad \vert \\ CH_2 \; \diagup CH_2 \\ CH_2 \end{array}$

- all cycloalkanes are also **saturated** hydrocarbons

- a **homologous series** is a family of compounds which can be represented by a general formula,
  e.g. the alkanes (C_nH_{2n+2}) and the alkenes (C_nH_{2n})

- successive members in a series differ in formula by a CH_2 group and hence relative molecular masses differ by 14

❏ there is a gradual change from one member of a homologous series to the next in physical properties,

e.g.   boiling point

❏ chemical properties of compounds in a homologous series are very similar due to all members having the same functional group,

e.g. the reaction of the alkenes with bromine

Alkynes

❏ the **alkynes** are another subset of the set of hydrocarbons

❏ the functional group in an alkyne is the carbon to carbon triple bond

❏ each member of the alkyne series has a name which ends in **-yne** and a prefix which indicates the number of carbon atoms in the molecule

❏ the general formula for the alkynes is C_nH_{2n-2} (each alkyne has four hydrogen atoms less than the corresponding alkane due to the triple bond),

e.g.

Number of carbon atoms in each molecule	Name of alkyne	Formula
2	ethyne	C_2H_2

Full structural formula	Shortened structural formula
H-C≡C-H	HC≡CH or CHCH

❏ all alkynes are also **unsaturated** hydrocarbons

Straight and branched chains

❏ in a **straight** chain all the carbon atoms are joined to one (at end) or two neighbouring carbon atoms,

e.g. CH_3-CH_2-CH_2-CH_2-CH_3

❏ in a **branched** chain one or more of the carbon atoms may be joined to three or four neighbouring carbon atoms,

e.g.   CH₃-CH-CH₂-CH₃
                |
              CH₃   **A**

              CH₃
               |
         CH₃-C-CH₃   **B**
               |
              CH₃

❑ when writing shortened structural formulae for branched alkanes, the branches are often put in brackets,

    e.g. $CH_3CH(CH_3)CH_2CH_3$ **A** $CH_3C(CH_3)_2CH_3$ **B**

❑ branches are names after the corresponding alkanes with the -ane ending changed to -yl,

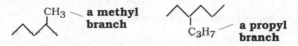

CH_3 **a methyl branch**

C_3H_7 **a propyl branch**

Systematic naming

❑ organic chemicals are given a systematic name according to an internationally accepted convention

❑ **to name a branched-chain alkane**

  (i)   select the longest continous chain of carbon atoms and name it after the appropriate straight-chain alkane

  (ii) number the carbon atoms from the end of the chain nearer the branch

  (iii) name the branch(es) and indicate the position(s) of the branch(es) on the chain,

e.g.

CH_3
$CH_3\text{-}CH_2\text{-}CH\text{-}CH_3$
  4   3   2 1

2-methylbutane
NOT
3-methylbutane

1 CH_3 3   4   5
2 $CH_2\text{-}CH\text{-}CH_2\text{-}CH_3$
        CH_3

3-methylpentane
NOT
1,2-dimethylbutane

1 CH_3
2 CH_2
$CH_3\text{-}CH\text{-}CH_2\text{-}CH_3$

3-methylpentane
NOT
2-ethylbutane

❑ cycloalkanes are named in a similar way,

  e.g. **methylcyclobutane**   **1,3-dimethylcyclohexane**

CH_3
$H_2C - CH$
$H_2C - CH_2$

CH_2 3
CH_2 $CH-CH_3$
CH_2 CH_2
1 CH 2
CH_3

❏ **to name an alkene**

(i) select the longest continous chain of carbon atoms containing the double bond and name it after the appropriate straight-chain alkene

(ii) number the carbon atoms from the end of the chain nearer the double bond and indicate the position of the double bond

(iii) name any branch(es) and indicate the position(s) of the branch(es) on the chain,

e.g.

CH_3-CH_2-CH=CH_2 CH_3-CH=CH-CH_3

   4   3   2   1   1   2   3   4

    but-1-ene   **but-2-ene**

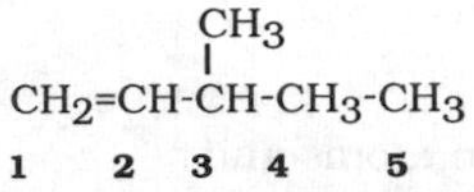

                  CH_3
                  |
CH_2=CH-CH-CH_3-CH_3

   1   2   3   4   5

  3-methylpent-1-ene

❏ **alkynes** are named in a similar way,

e.g.   **3-methylhex-1-yne**
                                  CH_3
                                 |
                CH≡C-CH-CH_2-CH_2-CH_3

                 1   2 3   4   5   6

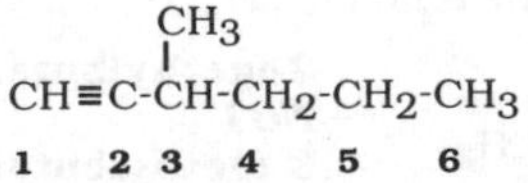

Isomers

❏ **isomers** are compounds with the same molecular formula but different structures

❏ the following flow diagram can be used to decide whether or not two compounds are isomers

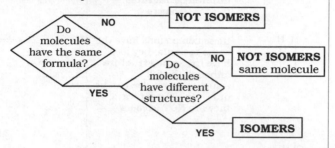

e.g.

CH₃-CH₂-CH₃	CH₃-CH₃	these compounds have **different formulae**; they are **NOT** isomers; **A** is propane **B** is ethane
A	**B**	

$$CH_3\text{-}CH_2\text{-}CH_3 \qquad CH_3\text{-}CH_3$$

these compounds have **different formulae**; they are **NOT** isomers; **A** is propane **B** is ethane

$$\begin{array}{c} CH_3 \\ | \\ CH_3\text{-}CH\text{-}CH_2\text{-}CH_3 \end{array} \qquad \begin{array}{c} CH_3\text{-}CH_2\text{-}CH\text{-}CH_3 \\ | \\ CH_3 \end{array}$$

C   **D**

these compounds have the **same formula** and the **same structure**; they are **NOT** isomers; they are both 2-methylbutane

$$\begin{array}{c} CH_3 \\ | \\ CH_3\text{-}C\text{-}CH_3 \\ | \\ CH_3 \end{array} \qquad \begin{array}{c} CH_3\text{-}CH\text{-}CH_2\text{-}CH_3 \\ | \\ CH_3 \end{array}$$

E   **F**

these compounds have the **same formula** but have **different structures**; they are isomers; **E** is 2,2-dimethylpropane **F** is 2-methylbutane

$$CH_2\text{=}CH\text{-}CH_2\text{-}CH_3 \qquad CH_3\text{-}CH\text{=}CH\text{-}CH_3$$

G   **H**

these compounds have the **same formula** but have **different structures**; they are isomers; **G** is but-1-ene

$$\begin{array}{c} CH_2\text{=}C\text{-}CH_3 \\ | \\ CH_3 \end{array} \qquad \begin{array}{c} CH_2\text{—}CH_2 \\ | \quad\quad | \\ CH_2\text{—}CH_2 \end{array}$$

I   **J**

these compounds have the **same formula** but have **different structures**; they are isomers, even though one compound is an alkene and the other a cycloalkane; **I** is methylpropene

- many compounds, other than hydrocarbons, have isomers,

e.g.

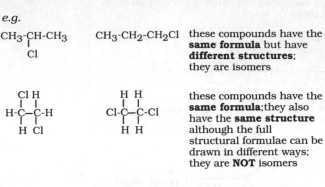

$CH_3\text{-}CH\text{-}CH_3$
  $\|$
  Cl
	$CH_3\text{-}CH_2\text{-}CH_2Cl$	these compounds have the **same formula** but have **different structures**; they are isomers

Cl H $\|$ $\|$ H-C-C-H $\|$ $\|$ H Cl	H H $\|$ $\|$ Cl-C-C-Cl $\|$ $\|$ H H	these compounds have the **same formula**; they also have the **same structure** although the full structural formulae can be drawn in different ways; they are **NOT** isomers
Cl Cl $\|$ $\|$ H-C-C-H $\|$ $\|$ H H	Cl H $\|$ $\|$ Cl-C-C-H $\|$ $\|$ H H	these compounds have the **same formula** but have **different structures**; they are isomers

Alkanols

- ethanol (found in alcoholic drinks) is the second member of a homologous series called the **alkanols**

- the alkanols are a subset of the set of **alcohols**

- the **hydroxyl** group (**-OH**) is the functional group in the alcohols

- each member of the alkanol series has a name which ends in **-anol** and a prefix which indicates the number of carbon atoms in the molecule,

e.g.

Number of carbon atoms in each molecule	Name of alkanol
2	ethanol

Full structural formula	Shortened structural formula
H H $\|$ $\|$ H- C-C-OH $\|$ $\|$ H H	$CH_3\text{-}CH_2\text{-}OH$ or CH_3CH_2OH

❑ from propanol onwards, isomerism can occur due to different positions of the hydroxyl group,

    e.g.   3   2   1   1   2   3

             $CH_3\text{-}CH_2\text{-}CH_2\text{-}OH$ $CH_3\text{-}CH\text{-}CH_3$

                                                     OH

❑ when writing structural formulae for alkanols in which the hydroxyl groups are not at the end of the carbon chain, the hydroxyl groups are put in brackets,

    e.g. $CH_3CH(OH)CH_3$

Naming alkanols

   (i)   select the longest continous chain of carbon atoms containing the hydroxyl group and name it after the appropriate alkanol;

   (ii) number the carbon atoms from the end of the chain nearer the functional group and indicate the position of the functional group;

  (iii) name any branch(es) and indicate the position(s) of the branch(es) on the chain,

    e.g.   3   2   1   1   2   3

             $CH_3\text{-}CH_2\text{-}CH_2\text{-}OH$ $CH_3\text{-}CH\text{-}CH_3$

                propan-1-ol   OH   **propan-2-ol**

          4   3   2   1

         $CH_3\text{-}CH\text{-}CH_2\text{-}CH_2\text{-}OH$ **3-methylbutan-1-ol**

               CH_3

❑ some alkanols have more than one hydroxyl group,

    e.g. $CH_2\text{-}CH_2$ $CH_2\text{-}CH\text{-}CH_2$

            OH OH   OH OH OH

         ethane-1,2-diol   **propane-1,2,3-triol**

          (ethylene glycol,   (glycerol)

        found in antifreeze)

Alkanals and alkanones

❑ ethanal is the second member of a homologous series called the **alkanals**

❑ the alkanals are a subset of the set of **aldehydes**

❑ alkanals take their name from the corresponding alkane; each member has a name which ends in **-anal** and a prefix which indicates the number of carbon atoms in the molecule

❑ the functional group in aldehydes is the **carbonyl** ($>$C=O); in aldehydes the functional group is always at the end of a carbon chain,

e.g.

Number of carbon atoms in each molecule	Name of alkanal
2	ethanal

Full structural formula	Shortened structural formula
H | H–C–C=O | | H H	CH$_3$-CH=O or CH$_3$CHO

❑ propanone is the first member of a homologous series called the **alkanones**

❑ the alkanones are a subset of the set of **ketones**

❑ alkanones take their name from the corresponding alkane; each member has a name which ends in **-anone** and a prefix which indicates the number of carbon atoms in the molecule

❑ the functional group in ketones is also the **carbonyl** ($>$C=O) but in ketones the functional group is always linked to two other carbon atoms ($-\overset{|}{\underset{|}{C}}-\overset{O}{\overset{||}{C}}-\overset{|}{\underset{|}{C}}-$),

e.g.

Number of carbon atoms in each molecule	Name of alkanone
3	propanone

Full structural formula	Shortened structural formula
H H | | H–C–C–C–H | || | H O H	CH$_3$-C-CH$_3$ || O or CH$_3$COCH$_3$

❏ from pentanone onwards, isomerism can occur due to the different positions of the carbonyl group; the carbon atoms are numbered from the end nearer to the functional group and the position of the functional group is indicated in the name,

e.g.

$$\overset{1}{C}H_3\text{-}\overset{2}{C}\text{-}\overset{3}{C}H_2\text{-}\overset{4}{C}H_2\text{-}\overset{5}{C}H_3 \qquad \overset{1}{C}H_3\text{-}\overset{2}{C}H_2\text{-}\overset{3}{C}\text{-}\overset{4}{C}H_2\text{-}\overset{5}{C}H_3$$
$$\quad\overset{\|}{O} \qquad\qquad\qquad\qquad\quad \overset{\|}{O}$$

pentan-2-one   **pentan-3-one**

Alkanoic acids

❏ ethanoic acid (found in vinegar) is the second member of a homologous series called the **alkanoic acids**

❏ alkanoic acids are a subset of the set of **carboxylic acids**

❏ alkanoic acids take their name from the corresponding alkane; each member has a name which ends in -**anoic acid** and a prefix which indicates the member of carbon atoms in the molecule

❏ the functional group in carboxylic acids is the **carboxyl**

group $\left(-C\overset{\displaystyle{\nearrow O}}{\underset{\displaystyle{\searrow OH}}{}}\right)$

❏ the functional group must always be at the end of a carbon chain,

e.g.

Number of carbon atoms in each molecule	Name of acid
2	ethanoic acid

Full structural formula	Shortened structural formula
H–C–C $\overset{\displaystyle{\nearrow O}}{\underset{\displaystyle{\searrow OH}}{}}$ with H above and H below the first C	CH$_3$-C $\overset{\displaystyle{\nearrow O}}{\underset{\displaystyle{\searrow OH}}{}}$ or CH$_3$COOH

Esters

❏ esters are covalent compounds with the molecules containing carbon, hydrogen and oxygen atoms

❏ esters have characteristic smells and are insoluble in water

❑ esters are the products of reactions between carboxylic acids and alcohols,

e.g. the reaction between ethanoic acid and methanol can be represented:

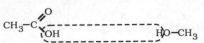

| | Note that the structure of the alkanol has been turned round |

acid : ethanoic acid   **alkanol : methanol**

⇅

ester   CH₃—C⟍O / O—CH₃   + H₂O

❑ since two reactants join up with the elimination of the elements to make water, the making of an ester is an example of a **condensation** reaction;
the reaction is also referred to as **esterification**

❑ the ' ⇌ ' sign shows that the making of an ester is a reversible reaction which can eventually reach equilibrium

❑ an ester takes its name from the alkanol and alkanoic acid from which it can be made,

e.g. alkanol : methanol   acid : ethanoic

    ester : **methyl**   ester : **ethanoate**

name : **methyl ethanoate**

structure :

CH₃—C⟍O / O—CH₃

from acid ' from alkanol

❑ since esters are prepared from alcohols and carboxylic acids, all esters contain the functional group:

—C⟍O / O—C—   (i)

from acid ' from alcohol

❑ when written the other way round, the functional group looks like:

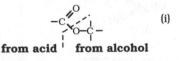

from alcohol   (ii)

    from acid

❑ esters can be represented in short as:

e.g.

$$CH_3C\,O\!\!\stackrel{\shortmid}{|}OC_2H_5 \quad \text{(i)} \qquad\qquad C_2H_5\,O\!\!\stackrel{\shortmid}{|}OC\,CH_3 \quad \text{(ii)}$$

from acid   from alkanol   from alkanol   from acid

❑ esters can be named from their structure,

e.g.   **from alkanol**   **from acid**

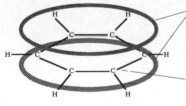

$$CH_3-CH_2-O\overset{\displaystyle \overset{O}{\|}}{\underset{|}{-C}}-CH_2-CH_3$$

| alkanol | : | ethanol | acid | : | propanoic |
| ester | : | **ethyl** | ester | : | **propanoate** |

name : **ethyl propanoate**

Aromatic hydrocarbons

❑ aromatic hydrocarbons are a subset of the set of hydrocarbons; they were so-called because of their distinctive fragrant smell (aroma)

❑ **benzene** is the simplest member of the class of aromatic hydrocarbons

❑ each carbon atom has three half-filled electron clouds involved in bonding with the neighbouring atoms

❑ one electron per carbon atom is not directly involved; these electrons are said to be **delocalised** (not tied to any one carbon atom)

delocalised electrons moving above and below the plane of the ring

planar ring of six carbon atoms

❑ the structure of benzene is often simplified to:

❑ in a substituted benzene ring the group of atoms represented by a -C_6H_5 group is called a **phenyl** group; thus   CH=CH$_2$ is called phenylethene

- the molecular formula for phenylethene is C_8H_8 (**not** C_8H_9 since one of the hydrogens in the benzene ring has been substituted)

- in a similar way, the molecular formulae for the following aromatic compounds are:

| aspirin | T.C.P. | T.N.T. |

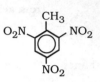

$$C_9H_8O_4 \qquad C_6H_3Cl_3O \qquad C_7H_5N_3O_6$$

3. REACTIONS OF CARBON COMPOUNDS

Cracking - revision

❑ the process of fractional distillation of crude oil does not produce sufficient petrol to meet present-day demands

❑ **cracking** is an industrial process which breaks up (cracks) the surplus of the heavier fractions into petrol

❑ when a catalyst is used to bring this about, the process is called **catalytic cracking**

❑ catalytic cracking can be carried out in the laboratory

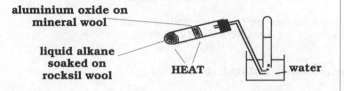

aluminium oxide on mineral wool

liquid alkane soaked on rocksil wool

HEAT

water

❑ to avoid 'suckback', the mouth of the delivery tube must be removed from the water before heating is stopped

❑ since all of the carbon to carbon bonds are equally strong cracking always produces a mixture of products, some of which are saturated and some of which are unsaturated,

$$e.g. \quad C_{24}H_{50} \rightarrow C_{12}H_{24} + C_{12}H_{26}$$

$$\rightarrow C_6H_{12} + C_{18}H_{38}$$

$$\rightarrow C_4H_8 + C_6H_{12} + C_{14}H_{30}$$

❑ in any one reaction the total numbers of carbon and hydrogen atoms in the product molecules always add up to the total numbers of carbon and hydogen atoms in the reactant molecule

Addition reactions - revision

❑ alkenes immediately decolourise bromine solution

❑ in the reaction of an alkene with bromine, the double bond breaks open and the two bromine atoms add on to the carbons on either side,

e.g.

$$\begin{array}{c} H \\ \diagdown \\ H \end{array} C=C \begin{array}{c} H \\ | \\ -C-H \\ | \\ H \end{array} + Br_2 \rightarrow H-\begin{array}{c} H \\ | \\ C \\ | \\ Br \end{array}-\begin{array}{c} H \\ | \\ C \\ | \\ Br \end{array}-\begin{array}{c} H \\ | \\ C \\ | \\ H \end{array}-H$$

propene

❑ this is called an **addition reaction**

❑ alkenes undergo addition reactions with hydrogen to form
the corresponding alkanes,

e.g.
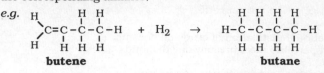

butene　　　　　　　　　　　　　　　　**butane**

❑ alkenes undergo addition reactions with hydrogen halides,

e.g.
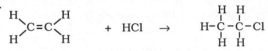

ethene　　　　　　　　　　　　　**chloroethene**

❑ alkenes have at least one carbon to carbon double bond;
the reactions of alkenes are a result of this functional
group

❑ alkanes and cycloalkanes do **not** undergo addition
reactions

Addition reactions - alkynes

❑ alkynes have at least one carbon to carbon triple bond;
the reactions of alkynes are a result of this functional
group

❑ alkynes can also undergo the addition of hydrogen,
hydrogen halides and halogens to form saturated
products

❑ there are two stages to the reactions,
e.g.

$$HC \equiv CH \quad \xrightarrow{Br_2} \quad \underset{Br}{\overset{H}{>}}C=C\underset{Br}{\overset{H}{<}} \quad \xrightarrow{Br_2} \quad H-\underset{Br}{\overset{Br}{C}}-\underset{Br}{\overset{Br}{C}}-H$$

ethyne

$$HC \equiv CH \quad \xrightarrow{H_2} \quad \underset{H}{\overset{H}{>}}C=C\underset{H}{\overset{H}{<}} \quad \xrightarrow{H_2} \quad H-\underset{H}{\overset{H}{C}}-\underset{H}{\overset{H}{C}}-H$$

$$HC \equiv CH \quad \xrightarrow{HCl} \quad \underset{H}{\overset{H}{>}}C=C\underset{Cl}{\overset{H}{<}} \quad \xrightarrow{HCl} \quad H-\underset{Cl}{\overset{H}{C}}-\underset{Cl}{\overset{H}{C}}-H$$

❑ the addition of bromine can be used to distinguish any
unsaturated hydrocarbon, either an alkene or an alkyne,
from a saturated hydrocarbon

Production of ethanol

❏ ethanol is produced by the **fermentation** of glucose; carbon dioxide gas is produced in the process; yeast contains the enzyme called zymase which catalyses the reaction

❏ to meet market demand, ethanol is made by methods other than fermentation; one industrial method involves the addition of water to ethene using a catalyst

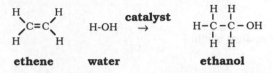

     ethene   **water**   **ethanol**

❏ this kind of reaction is called **catalytic hydration** or addition; the elements from water add on to the **one** molecule

Dehydration of alcohols

❏ ethanol can be converted to ethene by **dehydration**

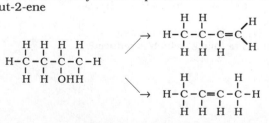

❏ this reaction which is the reverse of hydration, can be carried out in the laboratory

aluminium oxide on mineral wool

bromine solution is decolourised

ethanol soaked on mineral wool

HEAT

❏ butan-1-ol is dehydrated to produce only but-1-ene

❏ butan-2-ol is dehydrated to produce **both** but-1-ene and but-2-ene

Primary, secondary and tertiary alcohols

❏ to decide if an alcohol is primary, secondary or tertiary, look at the kind of atoms bonded to the carbon to which the hydroxyl group (-OH) is attached

❏ if **two** (or **three**) hydrogen atoms are attached to this carbon it is a **primary** alcohol; the hydroxyl group is always at the end of the chain

$$-\overset{\overset{\displaystyle H}{|}}{\underset{\underset{\displaystyle H}{|}}{C}}-\overset{\overset{\displaystyle H}{|}}{\underset{\underset{\displaystyle }{|}}{C}}-OH$$

❏ if **one** hydrogen atom is attached to this carbon it is a **secondary** alcohol

$$-\overset{\overset{\displaystyle H}{|}}{\underset{|}{C}}-\overset{|}{\underset{\underset{\displaystyle OH}{|}}{C}}-\overset{|}{\underset{|}{C}}-$$

❏ if there are **no** hydrogen atoms attached to this carbon atom it is a **tertiary** alcohol

$$-\overset{|}{\underset{|}{C}}-$$
$$-\overset{|}{\underset{|}{C}}-\overset{|}{\underset{\underset{\displaystyle OH}{|}}{C}}-\overset{|}{\underset{|}{C}}-$$

e.g.

propan-1-ol	$CH_3-CH_2-CH_2-OH$	**primary**
propan-2-ol	$CH_3-\overset{\overset{\displaystyle H}{|}}{\underset{\underset{\displaystyle OH}{|}}{C}}-CH_3$	**secondary**
2-methylbutan-2-ol	$CH_3-CH_2-\overset{\overset{\displaystyle CH_3}{|}}{\underset{\underset{\displaystyle OH}{|}}{C}}-CH_3$	**tertiary**

Oxidation

See
UNIT 2 PPA 1

❏ burning is an oxidation process; complete oxidation takes place in a good supply of oxygen; in a good supply of oxygen most alcohols burn to produce carbon dioxide and water,
e.g. *ethanol* + *oxygen* → *carbon dioxide* + *water*

❏ **primary** and **secondary** alcohols undergo oxidation using an oxidising agent

❏ **acidified potassium dichromate solution** is a suitable oxidising agent; the orange colour due to the dichromate ions changes to a blue-green colour due to the formation of chromium(III) ions in the reduction step

$$Cr_2O_7^{2-}(aq) + 14H^+(aq) + 6e^- \rightarrow 2Cr^{3+}(aq) + 7H_2O(l)$$

❏ oxidation can also be achieved by passing the alcohol vapour over **hot copper(II) oxide** (black) which is reduced to copper (brown)

$$Cu^{2+}(s) + 2e^- \rightarrow Cu(s)$$

❑ in each reaction the alcohol is oxidised in the corresponding oxidation step

❑ the product of the oxidation of a primary alcohol is an **aldehyde**

        primary alcohol → **aldehyde**

  e.g.   *methanol* → *methanal*

❑ a secondary alcohol is oxidised to form a **ketone**

        secondary alcohol → **ketone**

  e.g.   *propan-2-ol* → *propanone*

❑ a tertiary alcohol is **not** oxidised in this way

        tertiary alcohol ✗ **no reaction**

❑ oxidation can be considered to be loss of hydrogen as well as gain of oxygen; therefore, when applied to carbon compounds, oxidation results in an increase in the oxygen to hydrogen ratio

❑ the reverse reaction (reduction) can be carried out under suitable conditions; when applied to carbon compounds, reduction results in a decrease in the oxygen to hydrogen ratio

❑ aldehydes but **not** ketones can be readily oxidised by a suitable oxidising agent to produce a **carboxylic acid**

        aldehyde → **carboxylic acid**

  e.g. ethanal → ethanoic acid

        ketone ✗ **no reaction**

❑ **Fehling's solution** is a suitable oxidising agent

Making and breaking of esters

See
UNIT 2 PPA 2

❏ the making of an ester is an example of a **condensation** reaction

❏ in the reverse reaction, esters can be broken down to the alcohol and carboxylic acid by heating with an acid or an alkali,

e.g.

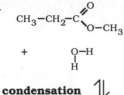

ester : methyl propanoate

$$+ \quad \overset{|}{\underset{H}{O}}-H$$

condensation ↑↓ **hydrolysis**

$$CH_3-CH_2-C\overset{\displaystyle O}{\underset{OH}{\diagup}} \qquad + \qquad HO-CH_3$$

acid : propanoic acid   **alkanol : methanol**

❏ since the breakdown of the ester occurs due to the addition of the elements of water, this is an example of a **hydrolysis** reaction

❏ the breakdown of an ester is also a reversible reaction which can eventually reach equilibrium

❏ an alkali is normally used to break down an ester in the laboratory,
e.g. sodium hydroxide solution

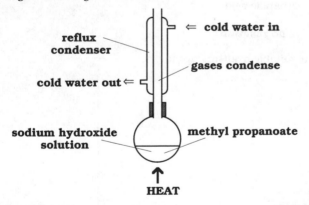

❏ the alkanol can be separated from the acid by **fractional distillation**

Percentage yields

❑ the yield in a chemical reaction is the quantity of a product obtained; the actual yield can be compared, as a percentage, with the theoretical yield

Example 1

5 g of methanol reacts with excess ethanoic acid to produce 9.6 g of methyl ethanoate.
Calculate the percentage yield.

balanced equation

$$CH_3OH \quad + \quad CH_3COOH \quad \rightleftharpoons \quad CH_3OOCCH_3$$

1 mol		1 mol
32 g	⟷	74 g
5 g	⟷	$\dfrac{74 \times 5}{32}$ g
	=	11.56 g

Theoretical yield $\quad = \quad$ 11.56 g

Actual yield $\quad = \quad$ 9.6 g

Percentage yield $\quad = \quad \dfrac{9.6}{11.56}$ x 100 $\quad = \quad$ **83%**

The percentage yield is an important consideration for industrial chemists.

Example 2

Under test conditions, 10 kg of nitrogen reacts with excess hydrogen to produce 1 kg of ammonia.
Calculate the percentage yield.

balanced equation $\qquad N_2(g) + \quad 3H_2(g) \quad \rightleftharpoons \quad 2NH_3(g)$

1 mol		2 mol
28 g	⟷	2 x 17 g
10 kg	⟷	$34 \times \dfrac{10}{28}$
	=	12.14 kg

Theoretical yield $\quad = \quad$ 12.14 kg

Actual yield $\quad = \quad$ 1 kg

Percentage yield $\quad = \quad \dfrac{1}{12.14}$ x 100 $\quad = \quad$ **8.24%**

4. USES OF CARBON COMPOUNDS

Competing demands

❑ crude oil is a **finite resource**, i.e. it is unable to be renewed

❑ many fuels are obtained by the **fractional distillation** of crude oil,

    e.g. petrol, diesel and paraffin

❑ consumer products are generally complex molecules which have been built up (synthesised) from small reactive molecules

❑ many consumer products, including plastics, textiles, detergents, dyes, cosmetics and agricultural chemicals, are made from carbon compounds produced from oil,

    e.g. the manufacture of plastics in the petrochemical industry is based on ethene as a starting material

❑ the competing demands for the use of crude oil is of industrial, economic and political importance

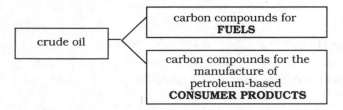

❑ aromatic compounds are particularly important in the manufacture of consumer products; one or more benzene hydrogen atoms can be substituted to form a wide range of carbon compounds,

    e.g. asprin, Kevlar, T.C.P.

Uses of esters and carboxylic acids

❑ many everyday substances are complex mixtures, with esters being important components

❑ the uses of esters tend to be based on their characteristics smells and the fact that they are good solvents for many covalent compounds,

    e.g. perfumes, food flavourings (smell), paint thinners and nail varnish (good solvents)

❑ carboxylic acids are also used in a variety of ways,

    e.g. ethanoic acid is found in vinegar, benzoic acid is a food preservative, terephthalic acid is used to make Terylene

Halogenoalkanes

❑ halogenoalkanes are compounds in which one or more of the hydrogen atoms in an alkane has been replaced by a halogen atom; chlorofluorocarbons (CFCs) contain chlorine, fluorine and carbon

❑ CFCs are very unreactive, have low flammability and low toxicity, properties which make them useful in a variety of consumer products; also the different family members have different boiling points which suit different applications

❑ CFCs have many everyday uses,

  e.g. as propellants in an aerosol can, as refrigerants in refrigerators and air-conditioning units, as blowing agents, as cleaning solvents

❑ ozone (molecular formula O_3) is a vital sunscreen gas which protects life on Earth from ultraviolet radiation

❑ it is thought that the extensive release of certain CFCs into the atmosphere could be a contributing factor in the destruction of the ozone layers and hence increasing ultraviolet radiation reaching the Earth

❑ this could lead to more cases of skin cancer and eye cataracts, could effect species such as plankton in the oceans and, in turn, other organisms involved in the food chain; also changes in the level of ultraviolet radiation reaching the Earth will affect the temperature of the Earth and in turn the weather

5. POLYMERS

Cracking again

❏ ethene and propene are starting materials of major importance in the petrochemical industry

❏ both ethene and propene can be formed by the cracking of naphtha, a product of the fractional distillation of crude oil

❏ ethene can also be formed by cracking ethane from natural gas

$$CH_3\text{-}CH_3 \quad \rightarrow \quad CH_2\text{=}CH_2 \quad + \quad H_2$$

❏ propene can also be formed by cracking propane from natural gas

$$CH_3\text{-}CH_2\text{-}CH_3 \quad \rightarrow \quad CH_2\text{=}CH\text{-}CH_3 \quad + \quad H_2$$

Manufacture of plastics - revision

❏ plastics are made of very long chain molecules; the large molecule is called a **polymer**; polymers are made by the joining together of small molecules; the small molecule is called a **monomer**; polymers made from unsaturated monomer units by the opening of carbon to carbon double bonds are called **addition polymers**; the process is called **addition polymersation**

❏ the name of the polymer is derived from the name of the monomer

Monomer	Polymer
ethene	poly(ethene)
propene	poly(propene)
styrene	polystyrene
vinyl chloride	polyvinylchloride (PVC)

❏ when thinking about addition polymerisation, it is useful to draw the alkene monomer in the shape of an ⊢ with the double bond in the middle,

e.g.

$$\begin{array}{ccc} H & & H \\ | & & | \\ C & = & C \\ | & & | \\ H & & H \end{array} \quad \text{for ethene, } CH_2\text{=}CH_2$$

$$\begin{array}{ccc} CH_3 & & H \\ | & & | \\ C & = & C \\ | & & | \\ H & & H \end{array} \quad \text{for propene, } CH_3\text{-}CH\text{=}CH_2$$

❑ molecules of ethene (a monomer) can join together by the breaking of the carbon to carbon double bonds to form poly(ethene) (a polymer)

$$\underset{\underset{H}{|}}{\overset{\overset{H}{|}}{C}}=\underset{\underset{H}{|}}{\overset{\overset{H}{|}}{C} \ + \ \overset{\overset{H}{|}}{C}=\overset{\overset{H}{|}}{C} \ + \ C=C \quad \rightarrow \quad -C-C-C-C-C-C-}$$

❑ the polymerisation of ethene can be represented as:

$$n \ \underset{\underset{H}{|}\ \underset{H}{|}}{\overset{\overset{H}{|}\ \overset{H}{|}}{C=C}} \quad \rightarrow \quad \left(\underset{\underset{H}{|}\ \underset{H}{|}}{\overset{\overset{H}{|}\ \overset{H}{|}}{-C-C-}} \right)_n$$

where n is a large number

❑ $-\overset{\overset{H}{|}}{\underset{\underset{H}{|}}{C}}-\overset{\overset{H}{|}}{\underset{\underset{H}{|}}{C}}-$ is called the repeating unit

❑ other polymers can be formed in a similar way,
e.g.

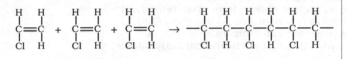

vinyl chloride   **polyvinylchloride**

❑ the processes involved in the production of plastics from crude oil are shown in the following flow diagram

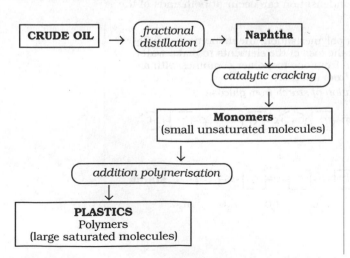

Polyesters

❑ polyesters are manufactured for use as textile fibres, *e.g. Terylene*

❑ the long polyester chains give the textile fibre a linear structure

❑ the fibres can be spun together to make a strong, flexible product used in the clothing industry

❑ polyesters are also manufactured for use as polymeric resins

❑ the acids used to make polyester resins are unsaturated and cross-linking with adjacent molecules produces a network structure

❑ this process, known as curing, produces a light, strong, rigid, product

❑ polyester resins are thermosetting polymers which are commonly mixed with glass fibre to form glass reinforced plastic, GRP; the resin is brushed on to the glass fibre and curing takes place at room temperature; GRP is widely used in boats, building panels and car body panels

Formation of polyesters

❑ **condensation polymers** are made from monomers with two functional groups in each molecule; the long chain is built up since condensation can occur at both ends of the molecule

❑ in condensation polymerisation, the monomers usually link together by the loss of the elements to make water; a hydrogen atom from one monomer combines with a hydroxyl group from another,
e.g. in the formation of starch from glucose

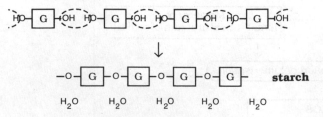

❑ **polyesters** are long chain molecules with many ester linkages

$$-\overset{O}{\underset{}{C}}-\blacksquare-\overset{O}{\underset{}{C}}-o-\square-o-\overset{O}{\underset{}{C}}-\blacksquare-\overset{O}{\underset{}{C}}-o-\square-o-\overset{O}{\underset{}{C}}-\blacksquare-\overset{O}{\underset{}{C}}-o-\square-o-\overset{O}{\underset{}{C}}-\blacksquare-\overset{O}{\underset{}{C}}-o-\square-o-$$

–■– and –□– represent different arrangements of carbon and hydrogen atoms

❑ polyesters are formed from alcohols with two -OH groups, one at either end of the molecules and acids with two

$-\overset{O}{\underset{}{C}}-OH$ groups, one at either end of the molecules; this means the polyester molecules can continue to grow in both directions

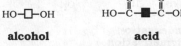

HO–□–OH $HO-\overset{O}{\underset{}{C}}-\blacksquare-\overset{O}{\underset{}{C}}-OH$

alcohol   **acid**

❑ the acid and the alcohol group can join together with the loss of water

↓ **condensation polymerisation**

$$-\overset{O}{\underset{}{C}}-\blacksquare-\overset{O}{\underset{}{C}}-o-\square-o-\overset{O}{\underset{}{C}}-\blacksquare-\overset{O}{\underset{}{C}}-o-\square-o-$$

Amines

❑ the **amines** are a homologous series of carbon compounds all containing nitrogen atoms

❑ the functional group in amines is the **amine** (or **amino**) group (-**NH$_2$**)

❑ each member of the series has a name which ends in -**amine** and a prefix which indicates the number of carbon atoms in the molecule,

e.g.

Number of carbon atoms in each molecule	Name of amine
2	ethylamine

Full structural formula	Shortened structural formula

H   H
   | |
H-C-C-NH$_2$
   | |
H   H
	CH$_3$-CH$_2$-NH$_2$
	or
	CH$_3$CH$_2$NH$_2$

Polyamides

❏ **polyamides** are formed from molecules with amine groups and carboxylic acid groups

amine group   carboxylic acid group

❏ the acidic and the amino groups can join together with the loss of the elements to form water

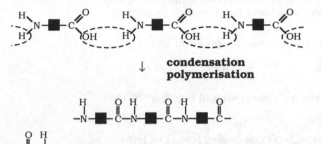

↓   **condensation polymerisation**

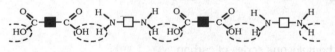

❏ the $-\overset{O}{\underset{}{\overset{\|}{C}}}-\overset{H}{\underset{}{N}}-$ link is called an **amide** link and the polymer is called a polyamide

❏ nylon is a polyamide that can be made from two different monomer units; one is a diacid and the other is a diamine

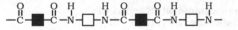

diacid   diamine

↓   **condensation polymerisation**

❏ in practice, nylon is made from the chloride of the acid rather than the acid

- the condensation involves the elimination of hydrogen chloride molecules

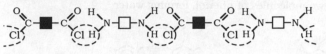

diacid chloride   **diamine**

↓ **condensation polymerisation**

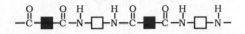

- the strength of nylon is related to the hydrogen bonding between the polymer chains

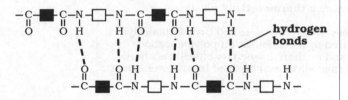

hydrogen bonds

Synthesis gas

- the steam reforming of methane from natural gas and the steam reforming of coal both produce **synthesis gas**

- synthesis gas is a mixture of carbon monoxide and hydrogen

- methanol is made from synthesis gas

- methanol can be oxidised to methanal which is a monomer for the manufacture of thermsetting plastics by condensation polymerisation

- this is an industrially important sequence of reactions

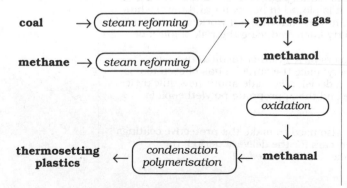

coal → (*steam reforming*) ── → **synthesis gas**

methane → (*steam reforming*) ╱ ↓

methanol

↓

(*oxidation*)

↓

thermosetting plastics ← (*condensation polymerisation*) ← **methanal**

- in the manufacture of bakelite the oxygen atom from a methanal molecule combines with two hydrogen atoms, one from each of two molecules of phenol, forming water

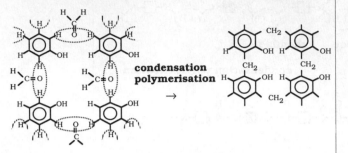

- the cross-linking of chains produces a highly rigid, three dimensional network which does not soften on heating; bakelite is therefore a **thermosetting** plastic

- a similar thermosetting plastic, called urea-formaldelyde resin, is produced by a condensation polymerisation involving urea and methanal; whereas bakelite is always brown, urea-formaldelyde can be dyed to whatever colour is required

- thermosetting plastics are used for heat resistant table tops and pot handles and in all types of electrical fittings, *e.g. plugs and sockets*

Unusual polymers

- the recent developments in polymer chemistry have led to the production of new plastics which have unique and interesting properties; these are related to their structures and bonding and give the polymers particular applications

- **poly(ethenol)** is an addition polymer which readily dissolves in water

- it is used to make laundry bags for hospitals; the bag dissolves when it is placed in hot water and the washing is released; this means that hospital workers do not need to handle the dirty linen, reducing the risk of infection

- dissolving polymers have another medical use - as stitches in surgery; once the surgeon has chosen to use soluble thread, a decision is made about how quickly it should dissolve and the appropriate poly(ethenol) is selected

- poly(ethenol) is also used to make the protective coatings which cover new cars for the delivery period; the dissolving polymer can be 'hosed off'

❑ poly(ethenol) is made by a process which involves ester exchange; methanol reacts with another polymer, poly(ethenyl ethanoate), to form the poly(ethenol) and a new ester, methyl ethanoate

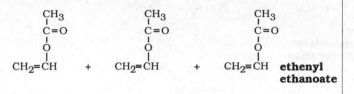

$$CH_3 \qquad\qquad CH_3 \qquad\qquad CH_3$$
$$C=O \qquad\qquad C=O \qquad\qquad C=O$$
$$O \qquad\qquad\quad O \qquad\qquad\quad O$$
$$CH_2=CH \quad + \quad CH_2=CH \quad + \quad CH_2=CH \quad \textbf{ethenyl}$$
$$\textbf{ethanoate}$$

↓   **addition polymerisation**

$$CH_3 \quad CH_3 \quad CH_3$$
$$C=O \quad C=O \quad C=O$$
$$O \qquad O \qquad O$$
$$-CH_2-CH-CH_2-CH-CH_2-CH_2- \textbf{ poly(ethenyl ethanoate)}$$

↓   **ester exchange**

$$OH \qquad OH \qquad OH$$
$$-CH_2-CH-CH_2-CH-CH_2-CH_2- \qquad \textbf{poly(ethenol)}$$

❑ **polyvinyl carbazole** is an addition polymer which exhibits photoconductivity - it conducts much better when light shines on it than when it is dark

❑ in many photocopying machines the photoreceptor surface, which is sensitive to light, is in the form of a metal drum coated with a very thin layer of this polymer

❑ **low density poly(ethene)** has a structure which can be modified to produce a photodegradable polymer - one which break up when exposed to sunlight

❑ carboxyl groups, which absorb light in the ultraviolet region, are introduced to the polymer chains; the trapped energy causes bonds to break in the neighbourhood of the carbonyl group, and the polymer chain breaks down into increasingly smaller pieces

- **Kevlar** is an aromatic polyamide formed by condensation polymerisation

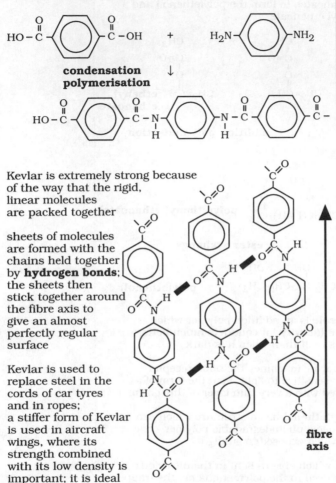

condensation polymerisation   ↓

- Kevlar is extremely strong because of the way that the rigid, linear molecules are packed together

- sheets of molecules are formed with the chains held together by **hydrogen bonds**; the sheets then stick together around the fibre axis to give an almost perfectly regular surface

- Kevlar is used to replace steel in the cords of car tyres and in ropes; a stiffer form of Kevlar is used in aircraft wings, where its strength combined with its low density is important; it is ideal for making bullet-proof vests and jackets for fencers are made from composites of Kevlar; leading racing motorcyclists wear protective suits containing Kevlar since the abrasion resistance of the polymer is better than leather; the use of Kevlar as a lining in aircraft holds to protect an aircraft from an explosion is presently being investigated

fibre axis

- **Biopol** is the trade name used by Zeneca for a family of natural polyesters made by certain bacteria

- Biopol is unusual in that the polymer is biodegradable, i.e. it can be broken down by bacteria found in the soil, in rivers and the sea

6. NATURAL PRODUCTS

Fats and oils

❏ the prime function of fats and oils in the diet is to provide energy

❏ fats and oils are a more concentrated energy source than carbohydrates

❏ a rough comparison could be made by burning different foods below a boiling tube containing water and recording the temperature rises

❏ fats and oils can be classified according to their origin

Animal	Vegetable	Marine
pork fat	sunflower oil	cod liver oil
beef fat	rape seed oil	whale oil
	palm oil	
	olive oil	

❏ there are differences between fats and oils

Fats	solid	more saturated molecules
Oils	liquid	more unsaturated molecules

❏ fats and oils are mixtures of molecules some of which are saturated and some of which are unsaturated

❏ the lower melting points of oils compared with fats are related to the higher proportion of unsaturated molecules in oils

❏ the saturated molecules are more closely packed; as a result, the van der Waals' forces of attraction between the molecules is relatively strong and so fats have relatively high melting points

❏ the shape of the unsaturated molecules in oils does not allow for close packing of the molecules; consequently the van der Waals' forces of attraction between the molecules will be weaker and hence the melting points of oils are lower than that of fats

❏ oils can be **hardened** to make them more suitable for use as margarine; partial removal of the unsaturation by the addition of hydrogen (hydrogenation) using a suitable catalyst raises the melting point

Structure of fats and oils

❑ fats and oils are examples of esters;
they can be broken up to produce different carboxylic
acids known as **fatty acids** and the one alkanol

❑ fatty acids are carboxylic acids containing chains of **even**
numbers of carbon atoms, ranging from C_4 to C_{24}, but
usually chain lengths C_{16} or C_{18}

❑ the carbon chains of the fatty acids can be saturated, e.g.
stearic acid, $C_{17}H_{35}COOH$, or unsaturated, e.g. oleic acid,
$C_{17}H_{33}COOH$

❑ in fats and oils, fatty acids are always
combined with propane-1,2,3-triol,
commonly called **glycerol**

$$CH_2-OH$$
$$|$$
$$CH\ -OH$$
$$|$$
$$CH_2-OH$$

❑ an alkanol with three -OH groups is called a trihydric
alkanol

❑ an ester formed from glycerol is called a triglyceride;
fats and oils consist largely of mixtures of triglycerides

❑ the three fatty acid molecules combined with each
molecule of glycerol may or may not be identical

$$
\begin{array}{l}
\quad\quad\ \ \overset{\displaystyle O}{\overset{\|}{}} \\
CH_2-O-C-R \\
|\quad\quad\ \ \overset{\displaystyle O}{\overset{\|}{}} \\
CH\ -O-C-R^* \\
|\quad\quad\ \ \overset{\displaystyle O}{\overset{\|}{}} \\
CH_2-O-C-R^{**}
\end{array}
$$

R, R*, R**, may or may not be
the same carbon chain

❑ hydrolysis of the triglyceride molecules produces glycerol
and the fatty acid(s)

$$
\begin{array}{l}
\quad\quad\ \ \overset{\displaystyle O}{\overset{\|}{}} \\
CH_2-O-C-R \\
|\quad\quad\ \ \overset{\displaystyle O}{\overset{\|}{}} \\
CH\ -O-C-R^* \\
|\quad\quad\ \ \overset{\displaystyle O}{\overset{\|}{}} \\
CH_2-O-C-R^{**}
\end{array}
$$

hydrolysis
$\rightleftharpoons$

$$CH_2-OH$$
$$|$$
$$CH\ -OH$$
$$|$$
$$CH_2-OH$$

glycerol

+

$$HO-\overset{\overset{\displaystyle O}{\|}}{C}-R$$

$$HO-\overset{\overset{\displaystyle O}{\|}}{C}-R^*$$

$$HO-\overset{\overset{\displaystyle O}{\|}}{C}-R^{**}$$

fatty acid (s)

❑ soaps are produced by the hydrolysis of fats and oils
using any alkaline solution; using sodium hydroxide
solution, the sodium salt(s) of the fatty acid(s) can be
produced as well as glycerol

$$R-\overset{\overset{\displaystyle O}{\|}}{C}-O^-\,Na^+$$

Proteins

- plants and animals need a supply of nitrogen to build proteins

- the nitrogen is usually taken in by the roots of plants as nitrate ions dissolved in water

- proteins are taken in by animals when plants or other animals are eaten

- animals need proteins as part of a balanced diet for body-building and repair

Structure of proteins

- the building blocks for proteins are amino acid molecules

- the structure of an amino acid molecule can be represented:

acid group   **amine (or amino) group**

- the represents the other arrangements of atoms in the various amino acids,

e.g.
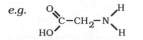   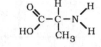

glycine   **alanine**

- the acidic group and the amino group of different amino acid molecules can join together with the loss of the elements to form water

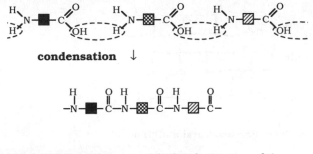

condensation ↓

- since two reactants join up with the elimination of the elements to form water, the making of a protein is an example of **condensation polymerisation**

❏ the 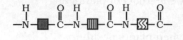 group is called a **peptide** link

❏ in the reverse process, protein molecules are broken down with the addition of the elements from water

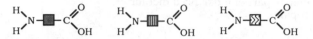

hydrolysis ↓

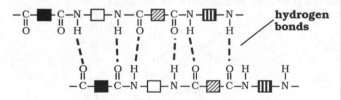

❏ since the breakdown of the protein occurs due to the addition of the elements from water, this is an example of a **hydrolysis** reaction

❏ proteins can be classified as **fibrous** or **globular**

❏ fibrous proteins are long and thin, a result of a linear structure based on the long polyamide chains

❏ intermolecular hydrogen bonding occurs between the carboxyl and amino groups

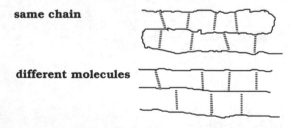

hydrogen bonds

❏ the hydrogen bonding can be within the same chain or between diferent molecules

same chain

different molecules

❏ fibrous proteins are the major structural materials of animal tissue,

e.g. *keratins - in hair, wool and nails,*
elastins - in lungs and arteries,
collagens - in skin and tissue

- intermolecular bonding in globular proteins can cause spiral chains which fold to give compact units

- globular proteins are involved in many human biological processes,

  e.g. enzymes, hormones (insulin) and haemoglobin

- protein molecules have a very high molecular mass since the molecules consist of long chains often with several thousand amino acid molecules joined together

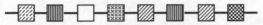

part of a 'protein' polymer

- there are over 20 different amino acids found in proteins; the different possible sequences of these amino acids allow for the wide variety of different protein molecules

- during digestion, insoluble protein in food is hydrolysed into amino acids; these smaller molecules can be absorbed into the bloodstream and taken to the various parts of the body to be reassembled in a different order to give the proteins that the body needs

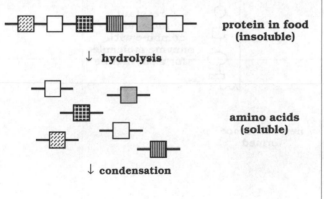

protein in food
(insoluble)

↓ **hydrolysis**

amino acids
(soluble)

↓ **condensation**

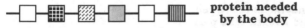

protein needed
by the body

- the body cannot make all the amino acids required for body proteins and is dependent on proteins in food for the supply of certain amino acids; these are known as **essential** amino acids

Enzymes

❑ biological catalysts are called **enzymes**

❑ enzymes speed up chemical reactions in living organisms,
e.g. during digestion, pepsin is the enxyme involved in the
hydrolysis of protein in foods to produce amino acids

❑ all enzymes are proteins

❑ it is thought that the shape of a molecule of enzyme
exactly complements the shape of the molecule upon
which it acts; this allows the two molecules to briefly
come together like a "lock-and-key", bringing about the
reaction,
e.g. a "building up" reaction

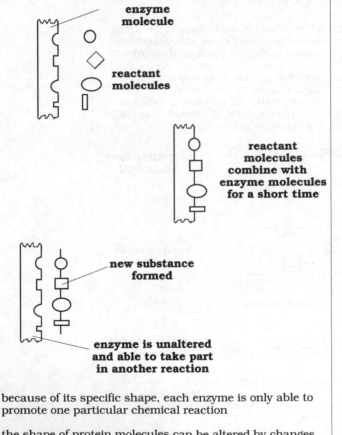

enzyme molecule

reactant molecules

reactant molecules combine with enzyme molecules for a short time

new substance formed

enzyme is unaltered and able to take part in another reaction

❑ because of its specific shape, each enzyme is only able to
promote one particular chemical reaction

❑ the shape of protein molecules can be altered by changes
in temperature and pH so that there is no longer a match
with the particular reactants;
this process is called **denaturing**

Enzyme activity

See
UNIT 2 PPA 3

❑ enzyme activity is extremely susceptible to changes in temperature and pH

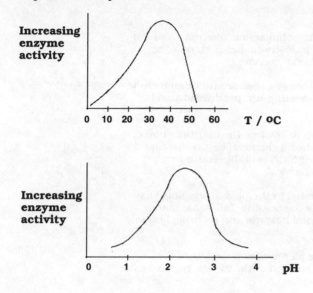

❑ each enzyme works best at a particular temperature and pH related to the conditions in which it normally operates; these are the **optimum conditions**; different enzymes have different optimum conditions

Unit 3   Chemical Reactions

1. THE CHEMICAL INDUSTRY

Introduction

❑   as well has having a major impact on the quality of our lives, the UK chemical industry makes a significant contribution to the national economy

❑   stages in the manufacture of a new product can include **research**, **pilot study**, **scaling-up**, **production** and **review**

❑   the research stage usually involves the identification of a new product with promising chemical behaviour and the development of the most likely suitable route for the manufacturing of the chemical

❑   the route is then evaluated in the pilot study stage using a small-scale version of the possible full-scale plant; health and environmental hazards and technical costs can be considered

❑   scaling-up involves the planning and design of the chemical plant taking account of the issues raised by the pilot study

❑   the new product is manufactured after the start-up of production

❑   as long as the plant is in operation, the process is reviewed with particular attention paid to ways of reducing costs and health and environmental hazards

❑   the major raw materials in the chemical industry are fossil fuels, such as oil and gas, metallic ores including bauxite (aluminium oxide), air, water and minerals such as salt (sodium chloride) and limestone (calcium carbonate)

❑   the raw materials are used as a source of **feedstocks**, i.e. the reactants from which other chemicals can be extracted or synthesised

❑ the chemical manufacturing processes usually involves a sequence of steps,

    e.g. typical steps for the manufacture of ammonia by the Haber Process are shown in the flow diagram

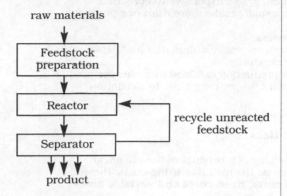

Batch or continuous

❑ the manufacturing may organised as a batch or as a continuous process

❑ with a batch process, after all the reactants have been used up, the plant must be shut down for the addition of fresh reactants to produce the same or different product(s)

❑ batch reactors are usually used to manufacture high purity chemicals which are required in relatively small amounts,

    e.g. pharmaceuticals, pesticides

❑ with a continuous process, fresh reactants can be constantly added to the plant, allowing the plant to operate for long periods of time without a shut down

❑ continuous reactors normally involve large-scale production; reactions tend to involve gases at high temperatures and often at high pressures with extensive use made of catalysts,

    e.g. manufacture of ammonia, catalytic cracking of hydrocarbons

❏   batch and continuous processes each have their
    advantages

    Batch process
    *   plant is generally less expensive to construct
    *   reactor can usually make more than one product

    Continuous process
    *   plant can be more easily automated and hence staffed
        by smaller workforce
    *   continuous production can lead to a cheaper product
        (provided plant is operating close to maximum
        capacity)

Economic considerations

❏   the economic viability of a product of the chemical
    industry depends on the manufacturing costs; these
    include **capital costs**, **fixed costs** and **variable costs**

❏   capital costs include those associated with the building of
    the chemical plant

❏   fixed costs include those associated with salaries and
    repayment of loans; these costs are likely to be the same
    irrespective of the output from the plant

❏   variable costs include those associated with plant output,
    e.g. the cost of raw materials, the cost of disposing of waste

❏   the UK chemical industry is, by and large, capital rather
    than labour intensive, i.e. plants which are expensive to
    build and run provide employment for a relatively small
    number of workers

❏   the energy released in exothermic reactions can be used
    to raise the temperature of reactants and hence reduce
    energy costs

Important factors

❑ the particular synthetic route which is chosen is also influenced by economic considerations,

   e.g. ethanoic acid can be prepared by:

   (a) *the bacterial oxidation of the ethanol in poor quality wines and beers; the cost of the raw materials is relatively cheap*

   (b) *direct oxidation of naphtha obtained by the factional distillation of crude oil; this method of producing ethanoic acid is only profitable because of the good markets for methanoic acid and propanoic acid, which are also formed in this reaction*

   (c) *the reaction of methanol with carbon monoxide; while the costs of feedstocks are low and the yield high, special materials are needed for plan construction leading to high capital costs*

❑ in practice, industrial operating conditions are chosen to maximise profit; often there has to be a compromise between factors such as yield, catalyst life and catalyst activity,

   e.g. increasing the pressure may increase the yield but could be over-costly, regularly renewing the catalyst may improve efficiency but this can be expensive, a more efficient catalyst may be available but if it is more expensive, profitability could be reduced

❑ the safety of the workforce is of the paramount importance to the industry,

   e.g. plant design is constantly improving to protect workers, there is strict legislation relating to exposure to harmful chemicals

❑ steps are also taken to ensure the safety of those who live near a chemical plant,

   e.g. flammable gases are burned off under controlled conditions to produce harmless gases

❑ environmental issues are also of major importance,

   e.g. discharge of harmful chemicals has been greatly reduced, chemicals are recovered and reused rather than treated as waste

❑ both historical and practical factors affect the location of chemical industries,

   e.g. many plants are situated close to the sea to ease import and export costs and disposal of effluent, new plants are often set up close to existing industries due to ready access to feedstock and skilled labour

2. HESS' S LAW

Conservation of energy

See
UNIT 3 PPA 1

❑ the law of conservation of energy states that energy can neither be created nor destroyed

❑ the application of the law of conservation of energy to chemical reactions is known as Hess's Law

❑ Hess's Law states that the enthalpy change in converting reactants into products is the same regardless of the route by which the reaction takes place,

e.g. the reaction

$$A \quad \rightarrow \quad B$$

may proceed by the three different routes

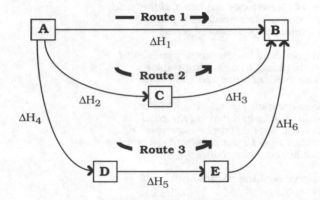

Total enthalpy change for Route 1 $\quad = \Delta H_1$

Total enthalpy change for Route 2 $\quad = \Delta H_2 + \Delta H_3$

Total enthalpy change for Route 3 $\quad = \Delta H_4 + \Delta H_5 + \Delta H_6$

According to Hess's Law the total enthalpy change for Routes 1, 2 and 3 will be identical,

i.e. $\quad \Delta H_1 \quad = \quad \Delta H_2 + \Delta H_3$
$$= \quad \Delta H_4 + \Delta H_5 + \Delta H_6$$

Applications of Hess's Law

❑ Hess's Law can be used to calculate enthalpy changes which are difficult or impossible to determine by experiment

Example 1

Calculate the entyalpy change for the reaction:

$$RbCl(s) \rightarrow Rb^+(g) + Cl^-(g)$$

Use the following enthalpy changes.

$RbCl(s)$	$\rightarrow$	$Rb^+(aq)$ +	$Cl^-(aq)$	$+17$ kJ mol^{-1}
$Rb^+(g)$	$\rightarrow$	$Rb^+(aq)$		-301 kJ mol^{-1}
$Cl^-(g)$	$\rightarrow$	$Cl^-(aq)$		-364 kJ mol^{-1}

Step 1 Write a balanced equation for the reaction the enthalpy change of which is to be found.

$$RbCl(s) \rightarrow Rb^+(g) + Cl^-(g) \quad \Delta H = ?$$

Step 2 Write a balanced equation for the reactions the enthalpy changes of which have been given and label them ΔH_a, ΔH_b, etc.

$RbCl(s)$	$\rightarrow$	$Rb^+(aq)$ +	$Cl^-(aq)$	ΔH_a
$Rb^+(g)$	$\rightarrow$	$Rb^+(aq)$		ΔH_b
$Cl^-(g)$	$\rightarrow$	$Cl^-(aq)$		ΔH_c

Step 3 Identify a second route for the reaction and label each step with the appropriate ΔH value, taking into account the number of moles involved and the direction of the reaction.

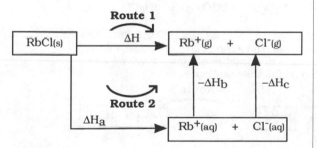

Note:

ΔH_b takes a negative sign since the reaction is reversed.

$$Rb^+(aq) \rightarrow Rb^+(g) \quad = \quad -(-301) \text{ kJ mol}^{-1}$$
$$= \quad 301 \text{ kJ mol}^{-1}$$

Similarly for ΔH_c.

Step 4 Apply Hess's Law.

The enthalpy change for the direct route, i.e. Route 1, will equal the total enthalpy change for Route 2.

$$\Delta H = \Delta H_a + (-\Delta H_b) + (-\Delta H_c)$$

Step 5   Substitute numerical values in the above
equation and solve for ΔH.

$$\Delta H = \quad +17 \; + \quad (+301) \quad + \quad (+364)$$

$$\Delta H = \; +682 \text{ kJ mol}^{-1}$$

i.e. $RbCl_{(s)} \quad \rightarrow \quad Rb^+_{(g)} \; + \; Cl^-_{(g)} \quad \Delta H = +682 \text{ kJ mol}^{-1}$

Example 2

Calculate the enthalpy change for the reaction:
$$2C_{(s)} \quad + \quad 3H_{2(g)} \quad \rightarrow \quad C_2H_{6(g)}$$
Take the enthalpies of combustion of carbon, hydrogen
and ethane to be -394 kJ mol^{-1} , -286 kJ mol^{-1} and
-1560 kJ mol^{-1} respectively.

Step 1   Write a balanced equation for the reaction the
enthalpy change of which is to be found.

$$2C_{(s)} \quad + \quad 3H_{2(g)} \quad \rightarrow \quad C_2H_{6(g)} \quad \Delta H = ?$$

Step 2   Write a balanced equation for the reactions the
enthalpy changes of which have been given and
label them ΔH_a, ΔH_b, etc.

$$C_{(s)} \quad + \quad O_{2(g)} \quad \rightarrow \quad CO_{2(g)} \qquad\qquad \Delta H_a$$
$$H_{2(g)} \quad + \quad O_{2(g)} \quad \rightarrow \quad H_2O_{(l)} \qquad\qquad \Delta H_b$$
$$C_2H_{6(g)} \quad + \quad 3^1/_2O_{2(g)} \rightarrow 2CO_{2(g)} \; + \; 3H_2O_{(l)} \quad \Delta H_c$$

Step 3   Identify a second route for the reaction and label
each step with the appropriate ΔH value, taking
into account the number of moles involved and
the direction of the reaction.

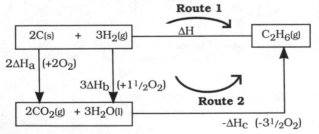

Note:

ΔH_a is multiplied by 2 since 2 mol of $C_{(s)}$ are involved.

Likewise, ΔH_b is multiplied by 3.

ΔH_c takes a negative sign since the reaction

$$2CO_{2(g)} \quad + \quad 3H_2O_{(l)} \quad \rightarrow \quad C_2H_{6(g)} \; + \; 3^1/_2O_{2(g)}$$

is the reverse of that for the enthalpy of combustion of
ethane.

Step 4   Apply Hess's Law.

The enthalpy change for the direct route, i.e. Route 1, will equal the total enthalpy change for Route 2.

$$\Delta H \;=\; 2\Delta H_a \;+\; 3\Delta H_b \;+\; (-\,\Delta H_c)$$

Step 5   Substitute numerical values in the above equation and solve for ΔH.

$$\Delta H \;=\; 2(-394) \;+\; 3(-286) \;+\; (+1560)$$

$$\Delta H \;=\; \textbf{-86 kJ mol}^{-1}$$

i.e. $2C_{(s)} \;+\; 3H_{2(g)} \;\rightarrow\; C_2H_{6(g)}$ $\mathbf{\Delta H = \text{-86 kJ mol}^{-1}}$

3. EQUILIBRIUM

Dynamic equilibrium

❑ most reactions are reversible; the forward and backward reactions occur at the same time and the reaction mixture contains both reactants and products

❑ if the conditions are not altered a balance point will be reached and the reaction will appear to have stopped; at this point the reaction has attained a state of **dynamic equilibrium**

❑ at equilibrium the rates of the forward and backward reactions are equal

❑ the sign ' $\rightleftharpoons$ ' is used to show that a reaction is at equilibrium,

e.g.   **A   +   B $\rightleftharpoons$ C   +   D**

❑ the changes in the concentrations of reactants and products as equilibrium is established can be summarised

start   **A + B** $\longrightarrow$

         A + B $\rightleftharpoons$ C + D

         A + B $\rightleftharpoons$ C + D

equilibrium A + B $\rightleftharpoons$ **C + D**

❑ at equilibrium **the concentrations of the reactants and the products will remain constant** but are unlikely to be equal

❑ if the concentrations of **A** and **B** are less than those of **C** and **D**, the equilibrium position lies to the right, i.e. to the side of the products

❑ if the concentrations of **A** and **B** are greater than **C** and **D** the equilibrium position lies to the left, i.e. to the side of the reactants

❑ the equilibrium position is the same regardless of whether it is approached from the reactant or product side

Factors which effect the position of equilibrium

(a) Concentration

❏ addition of reactant or removal of product will increase the rate of the forward reaction compared to the backward reaction; this will cause the equilibrium to shift to the right (product side); at the new equilibrium position the concentration of products will be higher

❏ addition of product or removal of reactant will decrease the rate of the forward reaction compared to the backward reaction; this will cause the equilibrium to shift to the left (reactant side); at the new equilibrium position the concentration of reactants will be higher

Example

$$Fe^{3+}(aq) \quad + \quad SCN^-(aq) \quad \rightleftharpoons \quad FeSCN^{2+}(aq)$$

Change in concentration	Direction in which equilibrium moves
$Fe^{3+}(aq)$ increase	to the right
$FeSCN^{2+}(aq)$ increase	to the left
$Fe^{3+}(aq)$ decrease	to the left

(b) Temperature

❏ increasing the temperature will increase the rate of both reactions but the one which removes heat will be favoured, i.e. the equilibrium will shift in the endothermic direction

❏ decreasing the temperature will decrease the rate of both reactions but the one which produces heat is not reduced as much, i.e. the equilibirum will shift in the exothermic direction

Example

$$N_2O_4(g) \quad \rightleftharpoons \quad 2NO_2(g) \quad \quad \Delta H \ +ve$$

Change in temperature	Direction in which equilibrium moves
increase	to the right
decrease	to the left

(c) Pressure

❑ increasing the pressure moves the equilibrium in the direction which reduces the number of gaseous molecules

❑ decreasing the pressure moves the equilibrium in the direction which increases the number of gaseous molecules

Example $N_2O_4(g)$ $\rightleftharpoons$ $2NO_2(g)$

Change in pressure	Direction in which equilibrium moves
increase	to the left
decrease	to the right

❑ changes in pressure will only effect the position of equilibrium if the equilibrium involves gas(es) and if there is a different number of moles of gaseous reactant(s) and product(s)

❑ a reaction involving gas(es) will only attain equilibrium if it is carried out in a closed container; if the container is open then the gas(es) will escape reducing the concentration of the gas(es)

Example
$CaCO_3(s)$ $\rightleftharpoons$ $CaO(s)$ + $CO_2(g)$

The decomposition of calcium carbonate will attain equilibrium in a closed container; in an open container, $CO_2(g)$ will escape and the equilibrium will continue to shift to the right until all $CaCO_3$ has decomposed.

The effect of a catalyst on the position of equilibrium

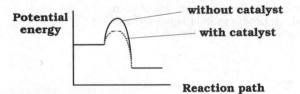

Potential energy — without catalyst — with catalyst

Reaction path

❑ if a catalyst is added there is the same decrease in the activation energies of the forward and backward reactions and the rates of both the forward and backward reactions will be increased

❑ a catalyst, therefore, does not alter the position of equilibrium

❑ although a catalyst does not increase the percentage conversion of reactants into products it does speed up the rate of attainment of equilibrium

Equilibrium in industry

e.g. *the industrial manufacture of ammonia by the Haber Process*

❏ the reaction is reversible and if the conditions were kept constant, equilibrium would be attained

$$N_2(g) + 3H_2(g) \rightleftharpoons 2NH_3(g) \quad \Delta H = -91 \text{ kJ mol}^{-1}$$

❏ conditions are carefully chosen to provide a compromise between fast production, a high yield of ammonia and low costs; factors which increase the rate of the forward reaction are favourable

(a) Concentration

❏ the Haber Process does not actually ever attain equilibrium due to the way the process is carried out

❏ in a condenser, the ammonia gas is cooled and the liquid ammonia piped off; constantly removing the ammonia gas decreases the rate of the backward reaction

❏ in addition, the unreacted nitrogen gas and hydrogen gas are recycled; the increase in the concentrations of the reactant gases increases the rate of the forward reaction

(b) Pressure

❏ since the number of product molecules is less than the number of reactant molecules, increasing the pressure increases the rate of the forward reaction compared to the backward reaction;the pressure chosen is about 200 atmospheres; beyond this pressure, the relative increase in the rate of the forward reaction can **not** justify the increased production costs

(c) Temperature

❏ since the reaction is exothermic, increasing the temperature decreases the percentage conversion of reactants to ammonia; increasing the temperature also increases the rate of both the forward and backward reactions; as a result the Haber Process is carried out at a moderately high temperature of about $400\,^{\circ}C$

(d) Use of a catalyst

❏ the catalyst will lower the activation energy for both the forward and backward reactions; using a catalyst therefore increases the rates of both the forward and backward reactions; this allows the process to be carried out more efficiently at a lower temperature

4. ACIDS AND BASES

Water

❑ in water there is an equilibrium between water molecules and hydrogen and hydroxide ions

$$H_2O(l) \quad \rightleftharpoons \quad H^+(aq) \quad + \quad OH^-(aq)$$

❑ the rate at which water molecules **dissociate** or **ionise** is equal to the rate at which hydrogen ions and hydroxide ions react to form water molecules

❑ since water is only a poor conductor of electricity, the equilibrium must lie to the left

The pH scale

❑ the pH of an aqueous solution is a measure of the concentration of hydrogen ions in that solution

❑ the relationship between hydrogen ion concentration and pH is:

pH = - (power to which the hydrogen ion concentration is raised)

❑ the pH of water and neutral solutions is 7

$$\therefore \quad [H^+(aq)] \quad = \quad 1 \times 10^{-7} \text{ mol } l^{-1}$$

where [ ] means 'concentration of '

❑ in water and neutral solutions:

$$[H^+(aq)] \quad = \quad [OH^-(aq)]$$

$$\therefore \quad [OH^-(aq)] \quad = \quad 1 \times 10^{-7} \text{ mol } l^{-1}$$

hence:

$[H^+(aq)] [OH^-(aq)] \quad = \quad 1 \times 10^{-14} \text{ mol}^2 \text{ } l^{-2}$

❑ this relationship holds true not only for water and neutral solutions but for all aqueous solutions

❑ the pH scale does not just extend from 0 to 14 but is a continuous range from below 0 to above 14

pH	[H$^+$(aq)] / mol l^{-1}		[OH$^-$(aq)] / mol l^{-1}	pH
15	1×10^{-15}		1×10^{1}	15
14	1×10^{-14}		1×10^{-0}	14
13	1×10^{-13}		1×10^{-1}	13
12	1×10^{-12}		1×10^{-2}	12
11	1×10^{-11}	**increasing alkalinity** ↑	1×10^{-3}	11
10	1×10^{-10}		1×10^{-4}	10
9	1×10^{-9}		1×10^{-5}	9
8	1×10^{-8}		1×10^{-6}	8
7	1×10^{-7}	**neutral**	1×10^{-7}	7
6	1×10^{-6}		1×10^{-8}	6
5	1×10^{-5}		1×10^{-9}	5
4	1×10^{-4}		1×10^{-10}	4
3	1×10^{-3}	**increasing acidity** ↓	1×10^{-11}	3
2	1×10^{-2}		1×10^{-12}	2
1	1×10^{-1}		1×10^{-13}	1
0	1×10^{0}		1×10^{-14}	0
-1	1×10^{1}		1×10^{-15}	-1

Example 1

State the pH of a solution with a hydrogen ion concentration of 10^{-2} mol l^{-1}.

$[H^+(aq)]$ $=$ 1×10^{-2} mol l^{-1}

pH $=$ **2**

Example 2

State the concentration of hydroxide ions in a solution with a pH of 5.

$[H^+(aq)]$ $=$ 1×10^{-5} mol l^{-1}

$[H^+(aq)][OH^-(aq)]$ $=$ 1×10^{-14} mol^2 l^{-2}

$[OH^-(aq)]$ $=$ $\dfrac{10^{-14}}{10^{-5}}$ $=$ **1×10^{-9} mol l^{-1}**

Strong and weak acids

❏   a **strong acid** is one in which all the molecules are
     dissociated (ionised) when dissolved in water,

     e.g. hydrochloric acid

$$HCl_{(g)} + {(aq)} \rightarrow H^+{(aq)} + Cl^-{(aq)}$$

     molecules   ions
     hydrogen chloride gas   hydrochloric acid

❏   a solution of hydrogen chloride gas will exist entirely as
     hydrogen and chloride ions; there will be no hydrogen
     chloride molecules present

❏   other strong acids include sulphuric and nitric acids

❏   a strong acid can be either concentrated or dilute
     depending on the number of moles of acid per litre of
     solution; the same applies to a weak acid

❏   a **weak acid** is one in which only some of the molecules
     are dissociated (ionised) when dissolved in water,

     e.g. ethanoic acid

$$CH_3COOH_{(aq)} \rightleftharpoons CH_3COO^-{(aq)} + H^+{(aq)}$$

     molecules   **ions**

❏   the functional group in carboxylic acids is the **carboxyl**

     group ($-C\overset{\displaystyle O}{\underset{OH}{\big\langle}}$)

❏   in solutions of carboxylic acids, there is limited
     dissociation of the -OH bond adjacent to the carbonyl
     group; an equilibrium is set up between the ethanoic acid
     molecules and the hydrogen and ethanoate ions;
     since the equilibrium position lies to the left, an ethanoic
     acid solution will exist mainly as molecules

❏   increasing the concentration of ethanoate ions
     will move the equilibrium to the left and increase the pH,

     e.g. by the addition of sodium ethanoate

❏   when comparing properties of strong and weak acids,
     solutions of equal concentration (equimolar) should be
     used

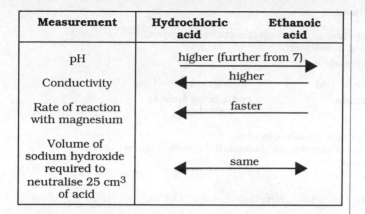

Measurement	Hydrochloric acid	Ethanoic acid
pH	higher (further from 7) →	
Conductivity	← higher	
Rate of reaction with magnesium	← faster	
Volume of sodium hydroxide required to neutralise 25 cm³ of acid	← same →	

❑ the pH is lower, the conductivity is higher and the rate of reaction with magnesium is faster with hydrochloric acid solution due to the reduced concentration of hydrogen ions, $H^+(aq)$, which results from the equilibrium in ethanoic acid solution

❑ the same volume of sodium hydroxide is required for neutralisation since the equilibrium continually shifts to the right, eventually producing the same number of hydrogen ions

❑ all carboxylic acids are weak acids,
   e.g. propanoic and citric acids

❑ other weak acids include carbonic acid (an aqueous solution of carbon dioxide) and sulphurous acid (an aqueous solution of sulphur dioxide)

carbonic acid
$$CO_2(aq) \quad + \quad H_2O(l) \quad \rightleftharpoons \quad 2H^+(aq) \quad + \quad CO_3^{2-}(aq)$$

sulphurous acid
$$SO_2(aq) \quad + \quad H_2O(l) \quad \rightleftharpoons \quad 2H^+(aq) \quad + \quad SO_3^{2-}(aq)$$

❑ both acids contribute to acid rain;
environmental damage is caused to iron structures and limestone ($CaCO_3$) by reaction with the hydrogen ions

$$Fe(s) \quad + \quad 2H^+(aq) \quad \rightarrow \quad Fe^{2+}(aq) \quad + \quad H_2(g)$$

$$CO_3^{2-}(s) \quad + \quad 2H^+(aq) \quad \rightarrow \quad CO_2(g) \quad + \quad H_2O(l)$$

Strong and weak bases

❑ a **strong base** is one in which all the available hydroxide ions are released in solution,

e.g. *sodium hydroxide*

$$Na^+OH^-{}_{(s)} \quad + \quad (aq) \quad \rightarrow \quad Na^+{}_{(aq)} \quad + \quad OH^-{}_{(aq)}$$

**sodium hydroxide
solid** **sodium hydroxide
solution**

❑ a **weak base** is made up of molecules;
only some of the molecules are dissociated (ionised) when dissolved in water,

e.g. *ammonia*

$$NH_3{}_{(aq)} + H_2O_{(l)} \rightleftharpoons NH_4^+{}_{(aq)} + OH^-{}_{(aq)}$$

molecules **ions**

❑ in ammonia solution, there is an equilibrium between the ammonium and hydroxide ions and the ammonia and water molecules; since the equilibrium position lies to the left, a solution of ammonia will exist mainly as molecules

❑ it is the lone pair of electrons on the nitrogen atom of the ammonia which results in the weakly alkaline solutions

❑ the lone pair of electrons attracts a hydrogen atom in a polar water molecule

**lone pair
of electrons**

❑ a bond is set up between the nitrogen and hydrogen atoms and at the same time, an O-H bond in the water molecule is weakened and eventually broken; in effect, hydrogen ions from water molecules are transferred on to some of the nitrogen atoms producing a solution which is rich in hydroxide ions and therefore alkaline

❑ increasing the concentration of ammonium ions will move the equilibrium to the left and decrease the pH,

e.g. *by the addition of ammonium nitrate*

- when comparing properties of strong and weak bases, solutions of equal concentration (equimolar) should be used

Measurement	Sodium hydroxide solution	Ammonia solution
pH	higher (further from 7) ←	
Conductivity	higher ←	
Volume of hydrochloric acid required to neutralise 25 cm^3 of alkali	← same →	

- the pH and conductivity are lower for the ammonia solution due to the lower concentrations of ions which results from the equilibrium

- the same volume of hydrochloric acid is required for neutralisation since the equilibrium continually shifts to the right, eventually producing the same number of hydroxide ions

pH of salt solutions

- salts derived from strong acids and strong alkalis dissolve in water to produce neutral solutions,

  e.g. sodium chloride

- salts derived from weak acids and strong bases produce alkaline solutions,

  e.g. sodium ethanoate

- when sodium ethanoate dissolves in water, it dissociates completely into ethanoate ions and sodium ions

  $CH_3COO^-Na^+(s)$ + (aq) → CH_3COO^- (aq) + $Na^+(aq)$

- the aqueous solution will also contain a few hydrogen and hydroxide ions due to the slight dissociation of water molecules

  $H_2O(l)$ ⇌ $H^+(aq)$ + $OH^-(aq)$

- ethanoate ions and hydrogen ions are found in ethanoic acid which is a weak acid and therefore exists mainly as molecules in aqueous solution; the ethanoate ions therefore react with the hydrogen ions to establish the equilibrium:

  $CH_3COO^-(aq)$ + $H^+(aq)$ ⇌ $CH_3COOH(aq)$

❑ as the concentration of hydrogen ions in the water equilibrium decreases, due to the ethanoic acid equilibrium, the water equilibrium shifts to the right

❑ as more hydroxide ions are produced, the pH increases

❑ salts derived from strong acids and weak bases dissolve in water to produce acidic solutions,

   e.g. ammonium chloride

❑ when ammonium chloride dissolves in water, it dissociates completely into ammonium ions and chloride ions

$$NH_4^+Cl^-(s) \quad + \quad (aq) \quad \rightarrow \quad NH_4^+(aq) \quad + \quad Cl^-(aq)$$

❑ there is an equilibrium between hydrogen ions and hydroxide ions and water molecules

$$H_2O(l) \quad \rightleftharpoons \quad H^+(aq) \quad + \quad OH^-(aq)$$

❑ ammonium ions and hydroxide ions are found in ammonia solution which is a weak base and therefore exists mainly as molecules in aqueous solution

❑ the ammonium ions therefore react with the hydroxide ions to establish the equilibrium:

$$NH_4^+(aq) \quad + \quad OH^- (aq) \rightleftharpoons NH_3(aq) \quad + \quad H_2O(l)$$

❑ as the concentration of hydroxide ions in the water equilibrium decreases due to the ammonia equilibrium, the water equilibrium shifts to the right

❑ as more hydrogen ions are produced, the pH decreases

Soaps

❑ soaps are formed by the alkaline hydrolysis of fats and oils,

   e.g. using sodium hydroxide

❑ since these compounds are esters of long chain fatty acids and glycerol, with these conditions, the sodium salts of the acids are produced

glycerol

sodium salts of fatty acid(s)

❑ soaps are therefore salts of weak acids and strong bases

5. REDOX REACTIONS

Oxidation and reduction

❑ **O**xidation **Is** the **L**oss of electrons by a reactant

❑ a metal element reacting to form a compound is an example of oxidation

O
I
L

❑ **R**eduction **Is** the **G**ain of electrons by a reactant

❑ a compound reacting to form a metal element is an example of reduction

R
I
G

❑ oxidation cannot occur without reduction, and vice versa

❑ oxidation and reduction reactions can be written as ion-electron equations

❑ ion-electron equations for reduction reactions can be found on page 11 of the Data Booklet,
e.g. $Cu^{2+}(aq) + 2e^- \rightarrow Cu(s)$

❑ to obtain ion-electron equations for oxidation reactions, the equations in the Data Booklet must be turned round,
e.g. $Mg(s) \rightarrow Mg^{2+}(aq) + 2e^-$

❑ redox reactions involve the transfer of electrons from one atom, molecule or ion to another

❑ to form the overall redox reaction, the ion-electron equations for the oxidation and reduction must be combined, ensuring that the number of electrons in the oxidation step cancels out with the number of electrons in the reduction step

Example 1

the reaction of magnesium with copper sulphate solution

oxidation $Mg(s) \rightarrow Mg^{2+}(aq) + 2e^-$

reduction $Cu^{2+}(aq) + 2e^- \rightarrow Cu(s)$

redox reaction $Mg(s) + Cu^{2+}(aq) \rightarrow Mg^{2+}(aq) + Cu(s)$

Example 2

the reaction of aluminium with dilute hydrochloric acid

oxidation $\qquad$ $Al_{(s)} \quad \rightarrow \quad Al^{3+}_{(aq)} \quad + \quad 3e^-$

reduction $\qquad$ $2H^+_{(aq)} \quad + \quad 2e^- \quad \rightarrow \quad H_{2(g)}$

To balance out the electrons, the oxidation must be multiplied by 2, and the reduction by 3.

$$2Al_{(s)} \quad \rightarrow \quad 2Al^{3+}_{(aq)} \quad + \quad 6e^-$$

$$6H^+_{(aq)} \quad + \quad 6e^- \quad \rightarrow \quad 3H_{2(g)}$$

redox reaction $\qquad$ $2Al_{(s)} \quad + \quad 6H^+_{(aq)} \quad \rightarrow \quad 2Al^{3+}_{(aq)} \quad + \quad 3H_{2(g)}$

❑ an **oxidising agent** is a substance which accepts electrons

❑ a **reducing agent** is a substance which donates electrons

❑ in the reaction of magnesium with copper sulphate solution, the $Mg_{(s)}$ is the reducing agent and the $Cu^{2+}_{(aq)}$ ion is the oxidising agent; in the reaction of aluminium with hydrochloric acid, the $Al_{(s)}$ is the reducing agent and the $H^+_{(aq)}$ ion is the oxidising agent

❑ ion-electron equations for reactions not included in the Data Booklet can be written from first principles

Example

Write the ion-electron equation for the reduction of dichromate ions to chromium(III) ions.

1. Write the formula for the reactant and product.
   $Cr_2O_7^{2-}_{(aq)} \qquad \rightarrow \quad Cr^{3+}_{(aq)}$

2. Balance the chromium.
   $Cr_2O_7^{2-}_{(aq)} \qquad \rightarrow \quad 2Cr^{3+}_{(aq)}$

3. Balance the oxygen by introducing the oxygen needed as water molecules. 7 mol of water will be needed on the RHS of the equation.
   $Cr_2O_7^{2-}_{(aq)} \qquad \rightarrow \quad Cr^{3+}_{(aq)} \quad + \quad 7H_2O$

4. Balance the hydrogen by introducing the hydrogen needed as hydrogen ions. 14 mol of $H^+_{(aq)}$ ions will be needed on the LHS of the equation.
   $Cr_2O_7^{2-}_{(aq)} \quad + \quad 14H^+_{(aq)} \rightarrow 2Cr^{3+}_{(aq)} \quad + \quad 7H_2O$

5. The electrical charge on each side of the equation must be balanced.

The nett charge on the LHS of the equation is 12+.
$$Cr_2O_7{}^{2-}(aq) \quad + \quad 14H^+(aq)$$
$$(2-) \quad + \quad (14+)$$

The nett charge on the RHS of the equation is 6+.
$$2Cr^{3+}(aq) \quad + \quad 7H_2O$$
$$2 \times (3+) \quad + \quad 0$$

Balance the charge by adding moles of electrons to the side which is more positive. 6 mol of electrons will be needed on the LHS of the equation.

$$Cr_2O_7{}^{2-}(aq) \; + \; 14H^+(aq) \; + \; 6e^- \; \rightarrow \; 2Cr^{3+}(aq) \; + \; 7H_2O$$

❑ redox reactions of this kind only take place in acidic solution - the $H^+(aq)$ ions are needed as a reactant

Volumetric titrations - revision

❑ the volume of acid (from a burette) required to neutralise a fixed volume of alkali (from a pipette) can be found using a suitable indicator to determine the end-point of the reaction

❑ if the concentration of the acid or the alkali is known then the concentration of the other can be calculated using the balanced equation

❑ in a neutralisation reaction, neutralisation is complete when all the $H^+(aq)$ ions from the acid have been removed by exactly the same number of $OH^-(aq)$ ions to form water,

i.e. number of moles   =   number of moles
of $H^+(aq)$ of $OH^-(aq)$

volume in litres   volume in litres
x   x
conc.   =   conc.
x   x
number of $H^+(aq)$ number of $OH^-(aq)$

OR multiplying both sides by 1000

volume in cm^3 volume in cm^3
x   x
conc.   =   conc.
x   x
number of $H^+(aq)$ number of $OH^-(aq)$

Example 1

What volume of NaOH(aq) (concentration 2 mol l^{-1}) is required to neutralise 50 cm^3 of HNO$_3$(aq) (concentration 1 mol l^{-1})?

number of moles of H$^+$(aq) = number of moles of OH$^-$(aq)

volume in litres		volume in litres
x		x
conc.	=	conc.
x		x
number of H$^+$(aq)		number of OH$^-$(aq)

$$50 \ \times \ 1 \ \times \ 1 \ = \ V \ \times \ 2 \ \times \ 1$$

$$V \ = \ \frac{50}{2} \ \text{cm}^3$$

$$= \ \mathbf{25 \ cm^3}$$

Example 2

If 25 cm^3 of H$_2$SO$_4$(aq) is required to neutralise 25 cm^3 of KOH(aq) (concentration 0.1 mol l^{-1}), what is the concentration of the H$_2$SO$_4$(aq)?

number of moles of H$^+$(aq) = number of moles of OH$^-$(aq)

$$25 \ \times \ \text{conc.} \ \times \ 2 \ = \ 25 \ \times \ 0.1 \ \times \ 1$$

$$\text{conc} \ = \ \frac{25 \times 0.1}{50} \ \text{mol } l^{-1}$$

$$= \ \mathbf{0.05 \ mol \ l^{-1}}$$

Redox titrations

See
UNIT 3 PPA 2

❑ the procedure used in volumetric titrations can be applied
to redox reactions, i.e. the concentration of a reducing
agent can be found using
(a) accurate volumes of the reactants,
(b) the known concentration of the oxidising agent,
(c) the balanced redox equation

Example

Iron(II) ions react with dichromate ions in acidic solution.
It was found that 21.6 cm^3 of dichromate solution
(concentration 0.1 mol l^{-1}), was required to oxidise
25 cm^3 of a solution containing iron(II) ions.

Equations

$Fe^{2+}(aq) \rightarrow Fe^{3+}(aq) + e^-$

$Cr_2O_7^{2-}(aq) + 14H^+(aq) + 6e^- \rightarrow 2Cr^{3+}(aq) + 7H_2O(l)$

Calculate the concentration of the iron(II) ion solution.

Step A
Calculate the number of moles of the oxidising agent, in
this case dichromate ions.

0.1 mol l^{-1} is 0.1 mol in 1 litre

0.1 mol ⟷ 1000 cm^3

$\underline{2.16 \times 10^{-3} \text{ mol}}$ ⟷ 21.6 cm^3

Step B
From the redox equation, calculate the number of moles
of iron(II) ions.

1 mol $Cr_2O_7^{2-}(aq)$ ⟷ 6 mol $Fe^{2+}(aq)$

2.16×10^{-3} mol ⟷ $\underline{1.30 \times 10^{-3} \text{ mol}}$

Step C
Calculate the concentration of iron(II) ions.

1.30×10^{-2} mol ⟷ 25 cm^3

0.52 mol ⟷ 1000 cm^3

i.e. the concentration of $Fe^{2+}(aq)$ ions is **0.52 mol l^{-1}.**

❑ as with volumetric titrations there has to be a way of determining the end-point of the reaction

❑ for some redox titrations the end-point can be recognised from a colour change involving one of the reactants,

  e.g. when potassium permanganate solution (purple) reacts with iron(II) sulphate solution, the permanganate ions are reduced to colourless manganese two-positive ions

Equations

$$Fe^{2+}(aq) \rightarrow Fe^{3+}(aq) + e^-$$

$$MnO_4^-(aq) + 8H^+(aq) + 5e^- \rightarrow Mn^{2+}(aq) + 4H_2O$$

purple   **colourless**

❑ at the end-point all the iron(II) ions have been oxidised and the excess permanganate ions cause the purple colour to remain

❑ when a colour change involving one of the reactants is used to indicate the end-point, the reaction is said to be **self-indicating**

❑ some redox titrations require an indicator,

  e.g. starch is used to detect excess iodine in the oxidation of vitamin C

Electrolysis

See
UNIT 3 PPA 3

❏ the production of one mole of an element from its ions, by electrolysis, always requires $n \times F$ coulombs, where n is the number of electrons in the relevant ion-electron equation, and F is the charge of one mole of electrons

Element	Ion-electron equation	Charge to produce one mole / coulombs
sodium	$Na^+ + e^- \rightarrow Na$	$\mathbf{1} \times 9.65 \times 10^4$
magnesium	$Mg^{2+} + \mathbf{2}e^- \rightarrow Mg$	$\mathbf{2} \times 9.65 \times 10^4$
aluminium	$Al^{3+} + \mathbf{3}e^- \rightarrow Al$	$\mathbf{3} \times 9.65 \times 10^4$
chlorine	$2Cl^- \rightarrow Cl_2 + \mathbf{2}e^-$	$\mathbf{2} \times 9.65 \times 10^4$
oxygen	$2O^{2-} \rightarrow O_2 + \mathbf{4}e^-$	$\mathbf{4} \times 9.65 \times 10^4$

❏ this quantity of electricity, 9.65×10^4 coulombs (96 500 coulombs), is called the Faraday, symbol F, after the original experimenter

9.65×10^4 coulombs $= 1$ Faraday

$\qquad\qquad\qquad\quad = $ charge of 1 mol of electrons

$\qquad\qquad\qquad\quad = $ charge of 6×10^{23} electrons

Example 1

A current of 10 A is passed through molten magnesium chloride for 15 minutes.

Calculate the mass of magnesium metal deposited at the negative electrode.

Quantity of electricity passed $\quad = $ current (A) x time (s)

$\qquad\qquad\qquad\qquad\qquad\quad = 10 \times 15 \times 60$

$\qquad\qquad\qquad\qquad\qquad\quad = 9000$ coulombs

Ion-electron equation $\qquad Mg^{2+} + 2e^- \rightarrow Mg$

Quantity of electricity required to produce one mole of magnesium from Mg^{2+} ions $\quad = \quad n \times F$ coulombs

$\qquad\qquad\qquad\qquad\qquad\qquad = \quad 2 \times 96\,500$ C

$2 \times 96\,500$ coulombs $\longleftrightarrow 24.3$ g (1 mol)

9000 coulombs $\qquad\longleftrightarrow 24.3 \times \dfrac{9000}{2 \times 96\,500}$

$\qquad\qquad\qquad\qquad\qquad\qquad = \mathbf{1.13\ g}$

Example 2

Aluminium is extracted from the molten ore using a current of 1.45×10^5 A.

How long will it take to produce 2.7 kg of aluminium?

$$1 \text{ mol} \quad \longleftrightarrow \quad 27 \text{ g}$$

$$100 \text{ mol} \quad \longleftrightarrow \quad 2700 \text{ g} \; = \; 2.7 \text{ kg}$$

Ion-electron equation $\qquad Al^{3+} + 3e^- \rightarrow Al$

Quantity of electricity required $\quad = \quad n \times F$ coulombs
to produce one mole of
aluminium from Al^{3+} ions $\qquad\quad = \quad 3 \times 9.65 \times 10^4$ C

Quantity of electricity required
to produce 100 mol of aluminium
from Al^{3+} ions $\qquad\qquad\qquad = 3 \times 9.65 \times 10^4 \times 100$ C

Quantity of electricity passed $\quad$ = current (A) x time (s)

$3 \times 9.65 \times 10^4 \times 100$ C $\qquad = 1.45 \times 10^5 \times$ time

$\qquad\qquad$ time $\qquad\qquad\qquad = \dfrac{3 \times 9.65 \times 10^4 \times 100}{1.45 \times 10^5}$

$$= \textbf{199.6 s}$$

Example 3

In the electrolysis of molten sodium oxide 2.3 g of sodium is deposited at the negative electrode.

Calculate the mass of oxygen produced at the positive electrode.

$$23 \text{ g} \quad \longleftrightarrow \quad 1 \text{ mol of sodium}$$

$$2.3 \text{ g} \quad \longleftrightarrow \quad 0.1 \text{ mol of sodium}$$

Ion-electron equation for reaction at the negative electrode

$$Na^+ \quad + \quad e^- \quad \rightarrow \quad Na$$
$$1 \text{ mol} \qquad\quad 1 \text{ mol}$$

hence ... $\qquad$ 0.1mol $\qquad$ 0.1 mol

$\qquad$ 0.1 mol of electrons have been used

Ion-electron equation for reaction at the positive electrode

$$2O^{2-} \quad \rightarrow \quad O_2 \quad + \quad 4e^-$$
$$1 \text{ mol} \qquad\quad 4 \text{ mol}$$

hence ... $\qquad\qquad$ 0.025 mol $\qquad$ 0.1 mol

$\qquad$ 0.025 mol of oxygen is produced

1 mol of oxygen (O_2) $\quad \longleftrightarrow \quad$ 32 g

0.025 mol $\qquad\qquad\quad \longleftrightarrow \quad \textbf{0.8 g}$

6. NUCLEAR CHEMISTRY

Atomic structure

❏ there are three sub-atomic particles

Particles	proton	neutron	electron
Symbol	$_1^1\text{p}$	$_0^1\text{n}$	$_{-1}^0\text{e}$
Approximate relative mass	1	1	0
Charge	1 positive	none	1 negative
Location	nucleus	nucleus	outside nucleus

❏ the **atomic number** is the number of protons in the nucleus of an atom of an element

❏ the **mass number** is the total number of protons and neutrons in the nucleus of an atom of an element

❏ **isotopes** are atoms of the one element with different numbers of neutron,
e.g. there are three isotopes of hydrogen

Name of isotope	protium	deuterium	tritium
Number of neutrons	0	1	2
Symbol	$_1^1\text{H}$	$_1^2\text{H}$	$_1^3\text{H}$

Radioactivity

❏ the stability of an atom depends on the relative numbers of protons and neutrons in its nucleus

❏ the lighter stable nuclei have approximately equal numbers of neutrons and protons but as the nuclei become heavier, the number of neutrons increases more rapidly than the number of protons

❏ the increase in the neutron to proton ratio with increasing atomic number is due to the neutrons playing a role in dampening the repulsive forces between the protons and thus preventing the nucleus from flying apart

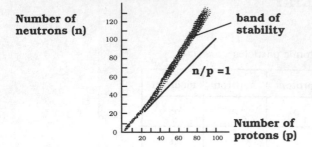

Number of neutrons (n) — Number of protons (p)

band of stability

n/p = 1

❑ **radioactivity** results from the nuclei of unstable isotopes of elements spontaneously disintegrating (**decaying**) with the emission of radiation and the release of energy

❑ radioactive decay alters the neutron to proton ratio with the release of energy and the process continues until the unstable radioactive nuclei form stable nuclei, i.e. nuclei with neutron to proton ratios which lie inside the stability band

❑ **radioisotopes** are isotopes which are radioactive

❑ in the radioactive decay process, changes take place in the nuclei of the radioisotopes; this is quite unlike ordinary chemical reactions where the nuclei remain intact and only the outer electrons are involved in the chemical changes

The nature and properties of radiation

❑ there are three types of radiation

Radiation	alpha	beta	gamma
Symbol	α	β	γ
Relative mass	4	very light	zero
Charge	2 positive	1 negative	none

❑ alpha and beta radiations are made up of particles

❑ the particles that make up **alpha** radiation are **helium nuclei** ($^4_2He^{2+}$) each containing two protons and two neutrons

- the particles in **beta** radiation are high energy **electrons** ($_{-1}^{0}$e) which are formed in the nucleus when neutrons break up

$$_{0}^{1}\text{n} \rightarrow {}_{1}^{1}\text{p} + {}_{-1}^{0}\text{e}$$

$$\textbf{neutron} \qquad \textbf{proton} \qquad \textbf{beta particle}$$

- **gamma** radiation consists of **electromagnetic waves**

- the three different types of radiation behave differently in an electric field

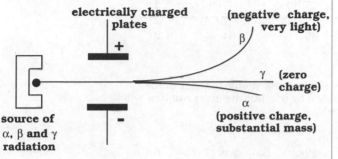

electrically charged plates

(negative charge, very light)

β

γ **(zero charge)**

α **(positive charge, substantial mass)**

source of α, β and γ radiation

- alpha, beta and gamma radiations also have different penetrating powers

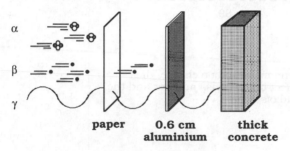

α

β

γ

paper **0.6 cm aluminium** **thick concrete**

Nuclear reactions

- when radioactive atoms disintegrate the changes which take place in the nuclei depend on the type of radiation emitted

- in balanced nuclear equations the total mass number on the left hand side of the equation is equal to the total mass number on the right hand side; the same is true for the atomic number

(a) alpha decay

❑ when a nucleus emits an alpha particle its atomic number will decrease by two (loss of two protons) and its mass number will fall by four (loss of two protons and two neutrons)

Example

Mass number   222   →   218   +   4

$$^{222}_{86}Rn \rightarrow \, ^{218}_{84}Po \, + \, ^{4}_{2}\alpha$$

Atomic number   86   →   84   +   2

(b) beta decay

❑ as a result of beta decay, the atomic number of the nucleus will increase by one but the mass number will remain unaffected

Example

Mass number   228   →   228   +   0

$$^{228}_{88}Ra \rightarrow \, ^{228}_{89}Ac \, + \, ^{0}_{-1}\beta$$

Atomic number   88   →   89   +   -1

(c) gamma decay

❑ since gamma rays have no mass and no charge, their emission will have no effect on the mass number and the atomic number of the radioisotope

Artificial radioisotopes

❑ bombarding a target of aluminium-27 with alpha particles results in neutron emission

$$^{27}_{13}Al \, + \, ^{4}_{2}\alpha \rightarrow \, ^{30}_{15}P \, + \, ^{1}_{0}n$$

❑ **neutron capture** can occur when neutrons are used as the bombarding particles

$$^{59}_{27}Co \, + \, ^{1}_{0}n \rightarrow \, ^{60}_{27}Co$$

❑ **proton capture** can occur when protons are used as the bombarding particles

$$^{14}_{7}N \, + \, ^{1}_{1}p \rightarrow \, ^{15}_{8}O$$

Half-life

❏ although the disintegration of the nuclei of radioisotopes is completely random the decay curves for all radioisotopes have a similar shape

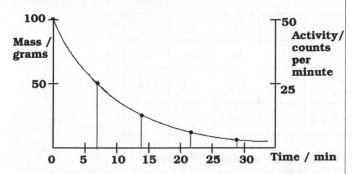

❏ the rate of decay depends only on the mass of the radioisotope present

❏ unlike ordinary chemical reactions it is not affected by changes in temperature or pressure or by the presence of a catalyst

❏ the time for a radioisotope to half its initial activity is known as the **half-life** (often abbreviated to $t_{1/2}$)

❏ it is also the time it takes for half the radioactive atoms initially present to disintegrate or the mass of the radioisotope to halve

❏ some radioisotopes have a very short half-life, others have very long half-lives,
e.g. radon-220 ($t_{1/2} = 55$ s),
uranium-238 ($t_{1/2} = 4.51 \times 10^9$ years)

❏ while the activity of a radioisotope depends on the mass present, the half-life of a radioisotope is independent of this, i.e. the time for half of a 1 kg sample of a radioisotope to decay is the same as the time for half of a 1 g sample of the same radioisotope to decay

❏ the half-life of a radioisotope is the same no matter whether the radioisotope is present as atoms of the element or as ions in a compound, i.e. the half-life of lead-206 in the element is the same as the half-life of lead-206 in $PbCl_2$

❏ this is because radioactive decay is a nuclear reaction and the formation of a compound involves only electrons and not the nucleus of an atom; the nucleus of an atom and its corresponding ion are identical

❑ a 3.2 g sample of phosphorus-32, half-life 14 days, decays by beta emission

$$^{32}_{15}P \quad \rightarrow \quad ^{32}_{16}S \quad + \quad ^{0}_{-1}e$$

Number of half lives	0	1	2	3
Time elapsed / days	0	14	28	42
Fraction of the original activity left	1	$1/2$	$1/4$	$1/8$
Mass of ^{32}P left / g	3.2	1.6	0.8	0.4

❑ using Avogadro's Constant, the number of ^{32}P atoms remaining after each half-life can be calculated

Number of ^{32}P atoms remaining	6×10^{22}	3×10^{22}	1.5×10^{22}	7.5×10^{21}

❑ each ^{32}P atom decays and produces a beta particle; the **total** number of beta particles produced can be calculated

Number of ^{32}P atoms decayed	0	3×10^{22}	4.5×10^{22}	5.25×10^{22}
Number of beta particles emitted	0	3×10^{22}	4.5×10^{22}	5.25×10^{22}

Example 1

A radioisotope of phosphorus has a half-life of 14 days. A sample of the radioisotope has a mass of 80 g.

Calculate the remaining mass of the sample of the radioisotope after 56 days.

Time to elapse   =   56 days
Half-life   =   14 days
Number of half-lives =   4

Time	Mass
0	80 g
$1 \times t_{1/2}$	40 g
$2 \times t_{1/2}$	20 g
$3 \times t_{1/2}$	10 g
$4 \times t_{1/2}$	**5 g**

Example 2

The initial radioactivity of a sample of a radioisotope was 100 counts/minute.
If the activity fell to 25 counts/minute in 24 days, what is the half-life of the radioisotope ?

Time	Activity in counts/minute
0	100
$1 \times t_{1/2}$	50
$2 \times t_{1/2}$	25

$$2 \times t_{1/2} = 24 \text{ days}$$
$$t_{1/2} = \textbf{12 days}$$

Example 3

A radioisotope has a half-life of 7×10^3 years.
How long will it take for 48 g of the radioisotope to decay to leave 6 g?

Time	Mass
0	48 g
$t_{1/2}$	24 g
$2 \times t_{1/2}$	12 g
$3 \times t_{1/2}$	6 g

$$t_{1/2} = 7 \times 10^3 \text{ years}$$
$$3 \times t_{1/2} = \textbf{2.1} \times \textbf{10}^\textbf{4} \textbf{ years}$$

Medical uses of radioisotopes

(a) To examine body tissues or organs
e.g. iodine-131 for thyroid gland

❑ the radioisotope is taken orally or injected; it travels to the organ in question; a camera records isotopic concentrations; overactive or underactive thyroid areas are shown up

(b) Implanted material
e.g. gold-198

❑ wire of the material is put directly into tumour; over next few days, isotope decays, dosing tumour

(c) Injected cancer treatment
e.g. iodine-131

❑ for thyroid gland as in (a), but the dose is designed to kill cancerous cells

(d) Irradiation of tumour

    e.g. cobalt-60, a powerful gamma source

❏   gamma rays are focussed onto the tumour site;
the tumour receives the dose while other tissues are hardly
affected

Industrial uses of radioisotopes

(a) Flaws in metal castings

❏   gamma radiograph of metal reveals flaws inside castings
(like X-ray of bone)

(b) Thickness control of steel

❏   gamma source is on one side of steel sheet and detector is
on other; if intensity falls, steel is too thick; if intensity
rises, steel is too thin; a computer controls steel thickness
from detector data

Uses of radioisotopes in scientific research

(a) Labelling of molecules

❏   scientists can follow the path of an atom from one
molecule to another by making a proportion of the
molecules from a radioactive isotope of the element,

    *e.g. phosphorus-32 in ammonium phosphate to find out
how plants use phosphorus*

(b) Carbon dating

❏   atmospheric carbon dioxide contains the radioisotope
carbon-14 which is formed when cosmic ray neutrons
bombard molecules of nitrogen

❏   since the rate of decay is the same as the rate of
formation there is a constant level of carbon-14 in the
atmosphere

❏   plants and animals have this same proportion as long as
they are living but once they die, they no longer take in
carbon-14 and so the level of radioactivity will decrease

❏   the proportion of carbon-14 left in a sample of carbon
taken from the plant or animal can be used with the
half-life of carbon-14 to determine the age of the sample

Example

Carbon from a wooden beam in an ancient tomb has an activity of 3.75 counts per minute per gram of carbon. New wood has an activity of 15.0 counts per minute per gram of carbon.

Two half-lives must have passed to reduce the activity from 15.0 to 3.75 counts and so the wooden beam must be 2 x 5600, i.e. 11 200 years old.

$$15.00 \quad \xrightarrow[t_{1/2}]{} \quad 7.5 \quad \xrightarrow[t_{1/2}]{} \quad 3.75 \text{ counts per minute}$$

i.e. two half lives

Energy production

(a) Nuclear fission

❑ during nuclear fission heavy nuclei split into lighter fragments

❑ the reactions are accompanied by an overall decrease in mass

❑ the mass loss is converted into energy which can then be harnessed

❑ to produce energy on a large scale the naturally occurring radioisotope uranium-235 can be bombarded by neutrons; one pattern of fragmentation is:

$$^{235}_{92}U \quad + \quad ^{1}_{0}n \quad \rightarrow \quad ^{90}_{38}Sr \quad + \quad ^{144}_{54}Xe \quad + \quad 2^{1}_{0}n$$

❑ the fission process is accompanied by the emission of more neutrons; these neutrons will cause fission in other uranium-235 nuclei and a chain reaction sets in

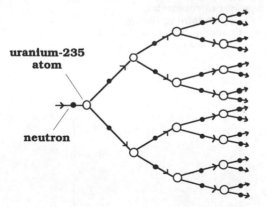

uranium-235 atom

neutron

❑ in a nuclear reactor the chain reaction is controlled by the absorption of some of the neutrons by non-fissionable material

❑ the large amounts of energy released in the fission of uranium-235 are used to generate electricity

❑ the artificial radioisotope plutonium-239 is the fuel in the more modern 'fast-breeder' reactors

❑ if the sample is above a critical size, uncontrolled fission leads to a nuclear explosion,

   e.g. in the atomic bomb

(b) Nuclear fusion

❑ in nuclear fusion two light nuclei fuse together to form a heavier nucleus

❑ elements are created in the stars from simple elements by nuclear fusion

❑ in the sun the nuclei of hydrogen atoms join together to produce atoms of helium; the process releases vast quantities of energy

$$^2H \quad + \quad ^2H \; \rightarrow \quad ^3He \quad + \quad ^1n$$

❑ the temperatures and pressures at the centre of the stars are so great that further fusion reactions take place to produce elements heavier than helium

❑ all naturally occurring elements, including those found in our bodies, originated in the stars

❑ nuclear fusion can only take place at extremely high temperatures which enable the nuclei to move fast enough to overcome the repulsion between them; this high temperature has been achieved in the thermonuclear "hydrogen bomb" but research is continuing to try to find a way of sustaining the high temperature and controlling the reaction so that it can be used as a plentiful, cheap source of energy

Nuclear and fossil fuels

❑ nuclear fuels and fossil fuels can be compared

Fossil fuels	Nuclear fuels
Safety	
many deaths to workers, e.g. mining accidents, accidents on oil platforms, incalculable damage to non-workers through air pollution, especially lung diseases	very few deaths to workers; concern over leukaemia in workers' children; leukaemia "clusters" near power stations, but no evidence of cause by nuclear industry;
Major accidents	
many in coal mining; Piper Alpha	Chernobyl; Windscale
Pollution	
coal tips; spoilage of land by open-cast mining; subsidence; air pollution, e.g. acid rain; oil spillages; global warming due to build up of carbon dioxide	fall-out from nuclear accidents; problem of disposal of nuclear waste, especially highly radioactive fission products; does **not** contribute to background radiation; does **not** contribute to global warming
Finite resources	
coal, oil and natural gas are all valuable sources of chemicals for manufacture of many products; supply of fossil fuels is limited	huge amounts of energy are made from very little uranium; use of breeder reactors would give supplies of nuclear fuel for the forseeable future; fusion would provide limitless supply of energy

UNIT 1   PPA 1   The Effect of Concentration
Changes on Reaction Rate

You should know:

❏ how to carry out an experiment to investigate the effect of concentration changes on reaction rate

❏ that reactions which are suitable will have a visible means of measuring the progress of the reaction, e.g. a colour change at the end of the reaction or when the reaction has gone a 'fixed distance'

❏ that concentration of one reactant is the only variable which is changed; all other variables are kept constant

Example
The reaction between hydrogen peroxide and an acidified solution of potassium iodide can be used to investigate the effect of concentration changes on reaction rate.

$$H_2O_2(aq) + 2H^+(aq) + 2I^-(aq) \rightarrow 2H_2O(l) + I_2(aq)$$

In the presence of sodium thiosulphate, the iodine produced is converted back to iodide ions.

$$I_2(aq) + 2S_2O_3^{2-}(aq) \rightarrow 2I^-(aq) + S_4O_6^{2-}(aq)$$

Starch indicator can be used to measure the time for the reaction to go 'a fixed distance'; once all the thiosulphate ions have been used up, a blue/black colour appears as iodine reacts with the starch.

Dilute sulphuric acid is used to acidify the potassium iodide solution.

The concentration of potassium iodide solution is changed by diluting with water; the total volume of solution is however kept constant.

The concentrations and volumes of all other solutions remain the same as does the temperature of the reactions.

For the different concentrations of potassium iodide, the time taken for the starch indicator to turn blue/black is noted and the rate is calculated; the shorter the time taken, the faster the rate of the reaction

Safety note:
Sulphuric acid is corrosive – splashes on the skin should be immediately washed off.

UNIT 1   PPA 2   The Effect of Temperature Changes on Reaction Rate

You should know:

❑   how to carry out an experiment to investigate the effect of temperature changes on reaction rate

❑   that reactions which are suitable will have a visible means of measuring the progress of the reaction, e.g. a colour change at the end of the reaction or when the reaction has gone a 'fixed' distance

❑   that temperature of the reaction is the only variable which is changed; all other variables are kept constant

Example

The reaction between oxalic acid and an acidified solution of potassium permanganate can be used to investigate the effect of temperature changes on reaction rate.

$$5(COOH)_2(aq) + 6H^+(aq) + 2MnO_4^-(aq)$$
$$\downarrow$$
$$2Mn^{2+}(aq) + 10CO_2(g) + 8H_2O(l)$$

A colour change of purple (due to permanganate ions, $MnO_4^-(aq)$) to colourless (as they are used up) can be used to indicate the end-point of the reaction.

Dilute sulphuric acid is used to acidify the potassium permanganate solution.

The temperature is changed by heating the reacting solutions.

The concentrations and volumes of all solutions are kept constant.

The temperature of the reacting solutions is recorded at the end-point of the reaction.

For each temperature, the time for the purple colour to "disappear" is noted and the rate calculated; the shorter the time taken, the faster the rate of the reaction.

Safety note:
Sulphuric acid is corrosive – splashes on the skin should be immediately washed off.

UNIT 1   PPA 3   Enthalpy of Combustion

You should know:

❏   how to carry out an experiment to allow an enthalpy of combustion to be calculated

Example

The enthalpy of combustion of ethanol is a suitable reaction.

(i)   Note the mass of a burner plus ethanol.

(ii)   Using a measuring cylinder, measure a fixed volume of water into a copper can and note the temperature of the water.

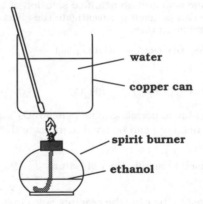

(iii) Place the burner under the can as shown and light the ethanol; it is useful to have a wind shield around the apparatus to prevent loss of heat.

(iv)   Stir the water and when the temperature has risen by approximately ten centigrade degrees, extinguish the flame and measure the highest recorded temperature of the water.

(v)   Reweigh the burner to find the mass of alcohol used.

The experimental value is less than the value in the Data Booklet because in this experiment it is assumed that **all** the heat energy from the burning is gained by the water; energy is however lost to the copper can and the surrounding air.

Safety note:

Ethanol is flammable – keep the bottle of ethanol away from flames.

You should know:

❏   how to distinguish between an aldehyde and a ketone

Example

Acidified potassium dichromate solution, Fehling's solution and Tollen's reagent are mild oxidising agents which can be used to distinguish between an aldehyde and a ketone.

With acidified potassium dichromate solution, a colour change of orange to blue/green indicates the aldehyde.

With Fehling's solution, a brick-red precipitate indicates the aldehyde.

With Tollen's reagent, the formation of a silver mirror indicates the aldehyde.

Test-tubes with reactants should be placed in a bath of boiling water.

Dilute sulphuric acid is used to acidify the potassium dichromate solution.

Safety note:
Aldehydes and ketones are flammable - heat in a water bath.

UNIT 2   PPA 2   Preparation of Esters

You should know:

❏   how to prepare and identify a simple ester

Example

Using heat and a suitable catalyst (concentrated sulphuric acid) a satisfactory yield of ester can be obtained.

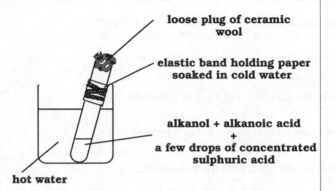

loose plug of ceramic wool

elastic band holding paper soaked in cold water

**alkanol + alkanoic acid
+
a few drops of concentrated sulphuric acid**

hot water

The paper soaked in water is to condense any vapour produced.

After heating, pour the mixture into a test-tube of sodium hydrogencarbonate solution to neutralise excess acid.

The ester, which separates to the top of the solution, can be detected by the characteristic smell.

Safety note:
Concentrated sulphuric acid is extremely corrosive – wear gloves when working with the acid;
alkanols are flammable – use a water bath for heating.

You should know:

❑   how to investigate the effect of pH or temperature change
    on enzyme activity

❑   that pH / temperature of the reaction is the only variable
    which is changed; all other variables are kept constant

Example

Catalase is an enzyme which catalyses the decomposition of
hydrogen peroxide into water and oxygen.

$$2H_2O_2(aq) \rightarrow 2H_2O(l) + O_2(g)$$

The number of bubbles of oxygen produced in a fixed time can
be taken as an indication of enzyme activity.

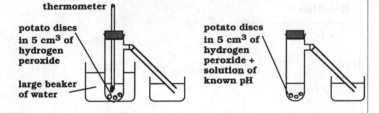

In each experiment, use the same number of potato discs, the
same volume of water and concentration of hydrogen peroxide
and ensure that the delivery tube is just under the surface of the
water.

The volume of hydrogen peroxide is measured using a syringe.

The temperature is changed by approximately 10 °C by heating
the water in the larger beaker and waiting until the temperature
of the water in the test-tube is constant before adding the
hydrogen peroxide.

The pH is changed using buffer solutions and an acid
(hydrochloric acid) and an alkali (sodium hydroxide solution).

Safety note:
Hydrogen proxide is an irritant - splashes on the skin should be
immediately washed off.

You should know:

❑   how to carry out an experiment to confirm Hess's Law

Example
Potassium chloride solution can be produced by two routes from solid potassium hydroxide.

Route 1 (Direct Route)
The reaction of dilute hydrochloric acid with potassium hydroxide solid.

Route 2 (Indirect Route)
Step a   The reaction of water with potassium hydroxide solid to form potassium hydroxide solution.

Step b   The reaction of dilute hydrochloric acid with potassium hydroxide solution.

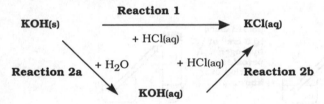

Reaction 1
(i)   Accurately weigh out potassium hydroxide into a plastic beaker.

(ii)   Using a measuring cylinder, measure out an excess of dilute hydrochloric acid into a second beaker and note the temperature (T_1).

(iii) Add the dilute acid to the potassium hydroxide, stirring continuously, and note the highest recorded temperature (T_2); the rise in temperature is $T_2 - T_1$.

Reaction 2a
(i)   Accurately weigh out potassium hydroxide into a plastic beaker.

(ii)   Using a measuring cylinder, measure out a fixed volume of water and note the temperature (T_1).

(iii) Add the water to the potassium hydroxide, stirring continuously, and note the highest recorded temperature (T_2); the rise in temperature is $T_2 - T_1$.

Reaction 2b

   (i)   Measure out an excess of dilute hydrochloric acid and note the temperature (T_1).

   (ii)   Note the temperature of the potassium hydroxide solution produced in Reaction 2a (T_2).

   (iii) Add the potassium hydroxide solution to neutralise the hydrochloric acid, stirring continuously, and note the highest recorded temperature (T_3);

the rise in temperature is $T_3 - \left(\dfrac{T_1 + T_2}{2} \right)$.

Allowing for experimental error, $\Delta H1 = \Delta H2a + \Delta H2b$.

Experimental error is mainly due to heat loss to the surroundings.

Safety note:
Acids and alkalis are corrosive - splashes on the skin should be immediately washed off.

You should know:

❏   how to make up a solution of known concentration

❏   how to carry out a redox titration

❏   how to determine the titre to be used in the calculation

❏   that the end-point in redox titrations can be determined
    using an indicator

Example

A solution of vitamin C can be oxidised using a solution of
iodine; starch solution, which turns a blue/black colour with
iodine at the end-point of the reaction, is used as the indicator.

(a)   Making up the vitamin C solution

(i)   Dissolve a vitamin C tablet in a little deionised water
      and add to the volumetric flask as shown.

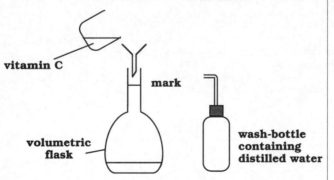

(ii)   Rinse out the beaker into the flask several times using
       deionised water from the wash-bottle.

(iii) Use the wash-bottle to add deionised water to make
       the volume up to the mark on the flask.

(iv)   Stopper the flask and shake several times to make
       sure the solution is thoroughly mixed.

(b) Carrying out the redox titration

(i) Using a pipette, add an exact volume of vitamin C solution to a conical flask.

(ii) Add a few drops of starch solution as indicator.

(iii) Note the initial volume of iodine solution in the burette.

(iv) Add the solution from the burette with gentle shaking of the flask; a colour change (in this case the formation of a blue/black colour which rapidly disappears on shaking) indicates the redox reaction is taking place.

burette

iodine solution

vitamin C solution + starch

white tile or paper

(v) Near the end of the reaction the colour disappears more slowly; at this stage add the iodine solution one drop at a time and note the volume added when the colour just remains.

(iv) Wash out the flask and repeat the titration until two consecutive results are within 0.1 cm^3 of each other; from these results determine the average volume of iodine solution used.

Typical results

	rough	accurate	
Initial volume / cm^3	0.0	20.4	0.0
Final volume / cm^3	20.4	39.8	19.5
Volume used / cm^3	20.4	19.4	19.5

The rough titre is ignored.

Average volume of solution = **19.45 cm^3**

Safety note:
Iodine solution "stains" the skin – splashes on the skin should be immediately washed off.

UNIT 3   PPA 3   Quantitative Electrolysis

You should know:

❑   how to determine the quantity of electricity required to
   produce one mole of hydrogen by electrolysis

Example

The electrolysis of a solution of dilute sulphuric acid
is a suitable experiment.

(i)   Assemble the apparatus and set the voltage source.

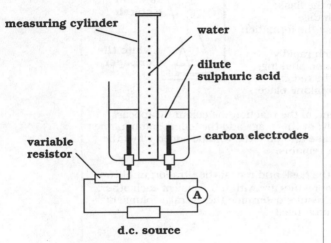

(ii)   Adjust the variable resistor to set the current; note the
   current and leave the current running through the
   solution for a few minutes.

(iii)   Position the graduated tube (or measuring cylinder)
   over the negative electrode making sure the tube (or
   cylinder) is not resting on the bottom of the cell.

(iv)   Switch on and pass the current for a fixed time;
   use the variable resistor to maintain a constant
   current if necessary.

(v)   Measure and record the exact volume of hydrogen
   produced in the fixed time.

Safety note:
Dilute sulphuric acid is corrosive – wear gloves when positioning
the graduated tube (or measuring cylinder);
hydrogen is flammable - make sure flames are absent when
releasing the gas at the end of the experiment.